New

Glass

A Worldwide Survey

This exhibition was organized by The Corning Museum of Glass

**Museums participating in
the New Glass exhibition**

The Corning Museum of Glass
Corning, New York
April 26, 1979–October 1, 1979

The Toledo Museum of Art
Toledo, Ohio
November 18, 1979–December 30, 1979

Renwick Gallery of the
National Collection of Fine Arts
Smithsonian Institution
Washington, D.C.
March 21, 1980–September 7, 1980

The Metropolitan Museum of Art
New York, New York
November 19, 1980–January 13, 1981

The Fine Arts Museums of San Francisco
California Palace of the Legion of Honor
San Francisco, California
March 28, 1981–June 14, 1981

This exhibition is supported in part
by a grant from the National
Endowment for the Arts in
Washington, D.C., a Federal Agency.

The quality of the exhibition
New Glass and its catalog has been
enhanced by the generosity of
Owens-Illinois and Owens-Corning
Fiberglas Corporation.

Printed in U.S.A.
Standard Book Number 0-87290-069-X
Library of Congress
Catalog Card Number 78-74015
Design: Anthony Russell and Melanie Roher
in collaboration with London Times Design
Photography: Raymond F. Errett and
Nicholas L. Williams
Printed by Sanders Printing Corporation, N.Y.C.

Pilkington
Presents
NEW GLASS

"New Glass" is presented by
the Pilkington Group
in conjunction with the
Victoria and Albert Museum.
It was organised by the
Corning Museum of Glass.

Table of Contents

Dedication

On the following pages the recent work of 196 artists, craftsmen/designers, and factories from twenty-eight countries is represented. The debt of gratitude we owe them is no greater than that due the 774 others who submitted slides and, in many cases, objects, who are not included. The exhibition is the direct result of their willingness to be judged and their generosity in making their work available. It is to all of the entrants that this catalog is dedicated.

Preface

This exhibition is about a profound change that is taking place in the history of glass: after thirty-five centuries of utilitarian use—from containers and window panes to television tubes and laser transmitting fibers—glass has become the amorphous substance from which functionless art is made. Suddenly, and in addition to its evolving roles in science, industry, housewares, and the crafts, glass has become a medium of the fine arts, a material in which to conceive and create—often directly—for purely aesthetic purposes.

Although the introduction of glassmaking to the art department curricula of more than a hundred schools, colleges, and universities is the single most identifiable reason for this phenomenal change—at least in the United States—there are others: improvements in melting technology, distribution of information, development of conceptual aesthetics, even the affluence of a society that can afford to produce both artists in glass and markets for their creations. There are also historic and geographic precedents that can, in retrospect, be credited for prophecy if not influence: Maurice Marinot and Jean Sala in France in the 1930's, and Edris Eckhardt in the United States in the 1950's are among the few who worked directly with hot glass; among the many post-war artist/designers whose impact continues to be felt, Pavel Hlava and the Libensky-Brychtová team in Czechoslovakia, Itoko Iwata and Kozo Kagami in Japan are of particular interest. But as occurs with most historic happenings, confusions and exceptions multiply as the works of specific people are considered. Are the schools where glass is taught in Art Departments turning out more craftsmen than artists? Is the glass made under the *direction* of an artist less significant than the glass made *by* an artist? Is glass produced by a machine bound to be different in aesthetic quality than glass made by hand even if the creative source is the same? What effect does function have on aesthetics in a material so traditionally associated with utilitarian vessels? Is "Studio Movement" a misnomer for glass' tardy incorporation in the craft renaissance? Whatever it is, is it having an influence on the glass industry?

This exhibition was conceived in an attempt to provide evidence from which answers to these and other questions could be drawn. The selection of objects represented a problem. If we followed the usual practice of inviting several authorities on glass to convene, establish criteria, and choose, we would be asking for judgments from within our specialized field at the very moment when glass is asking to be considered from outside—as art along with all the other media used in aesthetic expression. Furthermore, the idea of a jury agreeing on rules of judgment seemed unnecessarily limiting. Words governing, restricting, or even guiding personal sensibilities might result in the elimination of the fragile embryo of innovative insight, the real beginnings of change.

Finally, in an area ranging from borosilicate casseroles to expressions of social outrage, even the most sound judgmental criteria can become hopelessly inadequate. What happens to a non-utilitarian teapot measured against "form follows function"? Or to a mass-produced wineglass evaluated on the basis of its subject matter? We therefore abandoned the concept of a jury of glass experts in favor of four independent judges, each expert in making aesthetic distinctions, each from a different point of view: Franca Santi Gualteri, editor of *Abitare,* a magazine published in Milan, brought expertise in judging good design in housewares; Russell Lynes, former editor of *The Saturday Review,* author of *The Tastemakers,* is a New York based journalist specializing in the broad sweep of cultural history; Werner Schmalenbach, Director of the Kunst Museum in Düsseldorf, Germany, who has formed one of the finest collections of contemporary painting and sculpture in Europe, is a sophisticated critic of conceptual aesthetics; Paul Smith, Director of the Museum of Contemporary Crafts in New York City, U.S.A., specializes in the recognition of new talent—in glass as well as other media—with particular emphasis on the self-made.

Each of these people made selections independently without knowing the names of the entrants or the countries they represented, and the initials of each appear in close proximity to their choices both in the installation and in the pages that follow. Thus, this exhibition is what four very different people, all of whom make aesthetic visual judgments on a professional basis, think about contemporary glass.

From a glass specialist's point of view, at least that of The Corning Museum of Glass staff, reaction to the exhibition is exemplified by the many pieces acquired for our permanent collection; the number is limited only by available funds and avoidance of duplicating previously acquired objects. Although both quality and variety are as high and as rich as expected, the absence of particular artists, craftsmen, designers, and factories indicates that some did not submit their work to the exhibition; therefore the judges were not making comparisons over a full range of the best glass being made today. (See FSG's commentary on page 27.) Also evident is that while craft and art are bloom-

ing, the glass industry appears to be sitting relatively still. (See Russell Lynes'
commentary on page 29.) This may be because the changes elsewhere are so
novel and so evident that they overshadow the steady, more subtle improvements being made through design departments and such mechanical develop-
ments as centrifugal casting. The impact of today's artist in glass is bound to
eclipse the excitement generated by the industrial designer following World
War II just as that phenomenon eclipsed the personal exuberance of the Art
Nouveau and Art Deco giants of the previous era. When movements overlap,
only one can be most evident.

Although answers to the questions raised earlier in this preface must be
sought individually on the basis of the exhibition itself, it may be of interest to
note that the staff of The Corning Museum of Glass not only does not make
aesthetic distinctions between works done by hand, by machine, by artist, by
craftsman, or by designer; often we do not know which is which. After twenty-
eight years of collecting contemporary glass, however, we do know that it has
become a medium for the fine arts and that glass is being conceived, shaped,
and appreciated in ways radically different from anything ever done before in
its 3,500 year history.

Thomas S. Buechner
President and Director
The Corning Museum of Glass

*In order to give some sense of their attitudes if not criteria, each of the judges has provided a
short commentary for inclusion in this catalog. Also printed here are Antony Snow's account of
the organization of the exhibition, William Warmus' analysis of its content, and Russell Lynes'
summary of the two decades of change between the Museum's first survey of contemporary
glass, "Glass 1959," and the present exhibition. Mr. Lynes, also a judge on that occasion, brings
his perspective to this discussion.*

A Commentary

The purpose of these few comments is to chronicle the more important stages and decisions that influenced the final character of the *New Glass* Exhibition and its accompanying catalog. From the start, the organizers were keen to place as few limitations on the scope of the exhibition as possible so that the glass could be selected for its quality alone, whether made by hand or machine, individual or industry, in areas traditional or new to the world of glassmaking.

As we came face to face with the realities of the changes that had taken place since the first exhibition—for instance, approximately 6,000 slides were entered compared with 2,000 in 1959—our initial hopes and ambitions inevitably had to be curtailed. We were forced to limit the size of objects to no more than forty-eight inches (122 cm) in any dimension. We had to limit the number of entries to ten objects per individual and twenty per company. We had to ask entrants to bear the cost of transport and insurance of objects sent for the second stage of judging. Although The Corning Museum of Glass is exhibiting all objects selected by the judges as worthy of exhibition, the number was reduced to make a more practical traveling exhibition for the other institutions both in the United States and abroad. All these limitations and several more were accepted reluctantly by the organizers as they became aware of the high degree of interest by would-be exhibitors.

In May, 1976, glass artists and companies throughout the world were told of The Corning Museum of Glass' intention to mark the twentieth anniversary of its first Contemporary Glass Exhibition, held in 1959. Announcements of the exhibition were sent to glass magazines, universities, art schools, and all individuals known to have an interest in glass. The first stage of judging occurred in New York on June 26, 27, and 28, 1978. The 6,000 slides were submitted by 970 artists representing some twenty-nine countries. In three days the panel of four judges had to reduce this number to more manageable proportions; 950 entries were selected for the next stage of judging. On October 12, 13, and 14, 1978, in Corning, New York, the same panel was asked to judge either from the actual object if it had been sent to Corning, or, if the entrant preferred, from slides a second time. In a building temporarily, but specially, prepared for the receiving, customs clearance, unpacking, and storage of objects, the judges were able to view and compare the entries in their totality. Each object was also lighted individually either as the Museum staff elected or as the entrant had instructed. At this second stage, the judges reduced the number of objects to 427, which represented 196 entrants, 273 entries, and twenty-eight countries. The 273 entries finally selected are being exhibited first at The Corning Museum of Glass. All these objects are shown in this catalog, and one from each entrant is reproduced in full color.

The exhibition will be shown at The Corning Museum of Glass; The Toledo Museum of Art; The Renwick Gallery of the National Collection of Fine Arts, Smithsonian Institution; The California Palace of the Legion of Honor; and The Metropolitan Museum of Art before leaving the United States for England, France, and Japan.

In an exhibition of this scale, with such a long gestation period, mounted at a time when the staff of The Corning Museum were already watching the construction of their new Museum building and therefore forced to operate in temporary premises, no single individual amongst the small staff of twenty could avoid a most personal involvement. Especially to be thanked, therefore, are: Priscilla Price, Adrian Baer, and Joe Maio for their efforts in unpacking and display; Raymond Errett, Nick Williams and Charles Swain for their photographic work on the catalog under rushed and cramped conditions; publication supervision, Dr. John H. Martin and Charleen Edwards; the curatorial staff, Dwight P. Lanmon, Ernestine Kyles, Mark Malmendier, Todd Martin, and Katherine Poole. In particular, I would like to thank Darlene Schweiger who bore the full burden of mountains of paperwork over three years and Bill Warmus who joined the Museum staff halfway through the proceedings to become Assistant Curator, Twentieth-Century Glass. Lastly, I would like to thank all those outside the Museum both in the United States and abroad who gave constructive advice to help us overcome the many hurdles that had to be jumped before *New Glass* was a reality. I feel we have assembled an exhibition that truly represents as large an international glass community as possible and at the same time strengthens the claim of glass the material to be more highly regarded as a medium for aesthetic expression.

Antony E. Snow
Project Director
New Glass
The Corning Museum of Glass

Overview

Walking through the *New Glass* exhibition is like being in the center of a large crowd of varying posture: some objects are boisterous, some angry, others quiet, uniform, orderly. The material from which the exhibition was drawn is like the crowd, far too diverse to suggest a coherent theme; indeed, the selections of the four jurors, based upon their individual criteria, could be the basis for several exhibitions.

These notes are intended to identify some patterns within the "crowd" and some of the individuals represented. First, groups of objects are discussed in relation to one another as examples of a particular style. In the second section, specific techniques are considered as they relate to traditional approaches and as they make glassmaking easier for individual artists, designers, and craftsmen.

The prominence in *New Glass* of abstract, non-functional forms is a sharp change from *Glass 1959,* the first international exhibition organized by The Corning Museum of Glass. At that time a few individuals experimented with cut and engraved abstract forms, but aside from the works of Willem Heesen (fig. 1), Hanns Model (fig. 2), and Vicke Lindstrand (fig. 3), the vast majority of objects in the exhibition were functional forms or realistic images. This situation has changed markedly in twenty years. The "Genysys" series of Dan Bāncilá (plate No. 11), objects by Harvey Littleton (plate No. 126) and Marvin Lipofsky (plate No. 123), the works of Stanislav Libenský (plate No. 121) and Pavel Hlava (plate No. 81) as well as windows by Robert Kehlmann (plate No. 108) and Henry Halem (plate No. 71) are totally abstract. Just as functional objects such as cups and dishes would be abstract to anyone not familiar with utilitarian shapes, so these pieces may require association with images from the unconscious or ideas beyond consciousness to be understood.

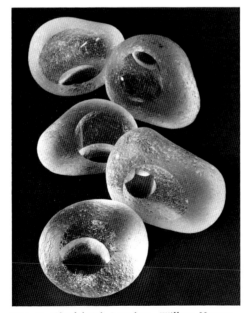

Fig. 1. *Glasfabriek Leerdam. Willem Heesen, designer. Five Stones, exhibited in* Glass 1959. *W. (approx.) 5.7 cm. Colorless glass, cut. The Corning Museum of Glass.*

Fig. 2. *Hanns Model, designer. Faceted block, exhibited in* Glass 1959. *H. 10.7 cm. Colorless glass, cut and engraved. The Corning Museum of Glass No. 61.3.324.*

Fig. 3. *Kosta Glasbruk AB. Vicke Lindstrand, designer. Prism, exhibited in* Glass 1959. *H. 5.0 cm. Pale blue tinted glass. Cut. The Corning Museum of Glass No. 58.3.64.*

In the abstract mode, quite another direction is taken by a group of pieces that utilize everyday materials such as sand and plate glass in ways that make the viewer think about them differently. Included here might be the work of Michelle Stuhl (plate No. 230) and Tom Armbruster (plate No. 5), as well as the various sculptural and geometric objects from Czechoslovakia, Hungary, and the United States that deal with the optical properties of cast or laminated glass.

As opposed to the cool geometry of much of the optical glass, some objects in *New Glass* are highly irregular in form and seemingly "unstructured." The sandblasted bowls of William Dexter (plate No. 50), Marvin Lipofsky's "Broken Basket Form" (No. 301), the lampwork of Věra Lišková (plate Nos. 124, 125), and James Harmon's vases (plate Nos. 74, 75) come to mind. The appeal of these works is manifest in the way they consciously deal with aspects of visual disorder. We might call them "informal," a term used by Herbert Read in his essay on *The Disintegration of Form in Modern Art:*

> *Informality, by which we generally mean <u>irregularity</u> of form, is not necessarily chaotic. Nature is full of organic forms that are super- ficially irregular. It may be that every form in nature—and there is no reason why we should confine our observations to organic forms—can be explained as the result of an interaction of forces, electro-magnetic or cosmic—that are measurable or predictable, but to the human eye, aided or not by the microscope, many of the structures of matter have an informal character. Such structures appeal to our aesthetic sensibility for reasons which we cannot explain—they fascinate us....The modern artist can create forms that are irregular in this sense and of similar attractiveness. The move- ment known as Abstract Expressionism is devoted to the exploration of this realm of irregular form, and there is no doubt that the individual artist can endow such forms with style and vitality...Even if they record no more than the graph of a gesture, the gesture, in so far as it is not aimless and therefore incoherent, is presumably sig- nificant: the calligraph records a state of mind.*[1]

Dalibor Tichý's forms (plate No. 237) and Lišková's lampwork are attractive in this way, while Lipofsky's "broken" sculpture is a reminder of that "other" side of glass, glass no longer fragile but fragmented *because* of its fragility and brittleness; it has become an awful, jagged shape revealing the shock of sharp, broken glass. Dale Chihuly's "Basket" series (plate No. 34) is also informal, with individual pieces "...reminiscent of old baskets which seem to be collapsing under their own weight" arrangeable and expandable into larger groups.[2]

Some objects in *New Glass* gesture for our immediate attention. They depend upon ready recognition of a familiar image only to distort that image and lead us into someone else's dream world. Erwin Eisch's finger series (plate No. 56) works its magic in "personifying" the finger as interpreter of pain, hope, love, birth, and death. John Cook (plate Nos. 41-43) makes primitive idols whose necks grow in length from one to the next; Ulla Forsell (plate No. 60) turns container shapes into a "Sky Castle." Others draw on regional motifs, as in the llama vase of the San Carlos Factory (plate No. 201) or the sculptures of Margarete Eisch. Ulrica Hydman-Vallien's enameled bowl (plate No. 87) and Bertil Vallien's "Captivity" (plate No. 242) are fairytales in glass.

The difficulties inherent in judging objects by sight alone are nowhere more evident than in the utilitarian objects. Here the visual aspect should be subordinate to function, but function need have no relation to appearance. Thus, a goblet must "feel" right in the hand, a group of cooking utensils must be easy to clean and to store in the cupboard, a teapot must have the handle placed so that the pot will be balanced when it pours. If the object also happens to be visually austere, we may come to feel that it is impersonal or "distant." Only constant, satisfactory *use* can overcome this sensation. Such is the case with the Jena tea set, (fig. 4) which first made its appearance in a design by Wilhelm Wagenfeld in the early 1930's and was subsequently refined into the form in *Glass 1959*.

Fig. 4. *Jena Glaswerk. Heinz Löffelhardt, designer. Tea set, exhibited in* Glass 1959. *H. of tea pot (approx.) 12.7 cm. Colorless glass, mold-blown. The Corning Museum of Glass.*

Mock functional objects continue to be popular in the United States. Richard Marquis' "Teapot" (plate No. 139), Robert Levin's "Cup with Appeal" (plate No. 120), and Audrey Handler's "Wedding Breakfast" (plate No. 72) all mimic functional forms with decoration and detailing so overwrought as to make the objects purely ornamental, like ritual artifacts from a lost culture. Băncilă's blue cut vases (plate No. 10) should also be considered among these artifacts; the sharp edges around the openings guard the interior like fangs and defy the insertion of a hand for cleaning. Erwin Eisch's glass "Telephone" (fig. 5) has long been a model for such pseudo-functional works.

Utilitarian forms like the Jena tea set (fig. 4) or Riedel's wineglass (plate No. 194) result from a series of subtle modifications over an extended period of time. Harvey Littleton's inverted tubes or the Fratelli Toso series of Marvin Lipofsky have undergone similar changes. However, it would seem that their studio pieces reveal not increasing precision and an approach toward a universal form, but rather a continuing search, with all its attendant uncertainties and insecurities, for the sources of individuality. Such works become rituals, and like rituals depend upon faith, not rational explanations for their continuation.

Glassmaking depends upon technologies which influence both the character of completed objects and the evolution of traditions. *New Glass* is itself an encyclopedia of those techniques, and a review of some of them may be instructive.

A number of objects, such as Anchor Hocking's (plate Nos. 3, 4), are machine made, blown on an automatic blowing machine. The vast majority of objects in the exhibition are, however, handblown, some in a novel manner. The vases of Tom Patti (plate No. 175) are made from laminated sheets of plate glass, softened and then blown. The lamination lines and an occasional applied line

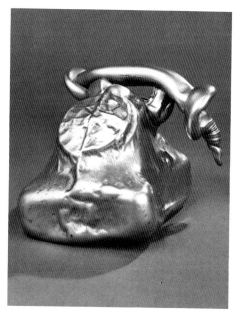

left
Fig. 5. *Erwin Eisch. Telephone, 1971. H. 15 cm. Colorless glass, mold-blown. Enameled. The Corning Museum of Glass No. 76.3.3.*

opposite, left
Fig. 6. *Maurice Marinot. Vase, 1924. H. 21.2 cm. Colorless glass, blown. Enameled. Acid-etched. The Corning Museum of Glass No. 51.3.123.*

opposite, right
Fig. 7. *Jean Sala. Bowl, ca. 1923. H. 8.1 cm, D. 10.3 cm. Opalescent glass with deep blue tinted glass decoration, blown. The Corning Museum of Glass No. 75.3.15.*

of color serve as a "grid," describing the form and progress of the air bubble at the point of solidification of the glass. Gunnar Cyrén uses the Graal technique developed in 1916 by Simon Gate at Orrefors Glasbruk. The process involves cutting a pattern in the glass; the object is then heated and cased with colorless glass, producing a "soft-focus" image.

Techniques of surface abrasion range from the eccentric realism of Jiři Harcuba's engraving (plate No. 73) to the massive cut features of Michael Esson's "Self Portrait" (plate No. 58). There are works by Ann Wärff (plate Nos. 261-2) that combine sandblasting and multiple layers of etched colored glass into a fantasy suggesting palm trees and office chairs, a curious blend of Art Deco and the surreal; sandblasted and polished bowls by Vízner that seem like three-dimensional shadows that cease to exist when the lights go out; and pressed, partially sandblasted dishes by Funakoshi (plate No. 63) that create images of islands floating on the surface where the objects come to rest. It should be noted that while sandblasting has long been used to mask the character of an impure glass, it is used today to enhance the visual quality of some very fine glass such as that of Funakoshi or Vízner. At the same time, many artists have recently used the stones (solid impurities), blisters (bubbles), and cords (variations in the optical qualities and density of the glass) as decorative or textural elements.

Of the possible technical innovations, those most often adopted by studio artists enable individuals to produce glass alone and unaided. Such individuals were already at work in the 1920's and 1930's, notably in France. Maurice Marinot (fig. 6) is often cited as a leading influence by contemporary glassmakers, as is Jean Sala (fig. 7). So it is not without interest that Sala was once regarded as "...one of the last of the authentic glassmakers, that is, men who carry out their ideas personally, thereby adding to the beauty of the original conception the peculiar charm of rapid, inspired and spontaneous improvisa-

tion, for which practical knowledge is after all necessary."[3] What reversals forty years may bring! While Sala was seen as the end of a tradition, we now see him as a forerunner of the studio movement that started in America in the early 1960's.

It was at that time that Harvey Littleton, Tom McGlauchlin (represented by the object in plate No. 144), and others began a series of glass workshops at the Toledo Museum of Art.[4] Dominick Labino (represented by the object in plate No. 119) contributed materials for the program, including a formula for a low-melting-temperature glass. As a result glass can be used as an individual medium similar to oil paints, ceramics, and textiles. Small furnaces, advances in refractory technology (the furnace materials that contain the molten glass) and the availability of standardized materials in open stock such as compatible colors, rods of glass (with the same coefficients of expansion) of every possible hue, have encouraged this development. Glassmaking programs throughout the United States have also been important. Courses were set up at the Toledo Museum in 1967 (by Fritz Dreisbach), the University of Wisconsin at Madison in 1962-1963 (Harvey Littleton), and Alfred University in 1968-1969 (André Billeci). Marvin Lipofsky established a glassmaking program at the University of California at Berkeley in 1964, and is now head of the department at the California College of Arts and Crafts. Today glassmaking is taught throughout the United States at institutions such as the Rhode Island School of Design (Dale Chihuly), Kent State University (Henry Halem), Illinois State University (Joel Myers), and the Tyler School of Art at Temple University (Jon Clark). Craft schools with recognized studio glass programs include the Pilchuck Glass Center in Washington, The Penland School of Arts and Crafts in North Carolina, and the Haystack Mountain School of Crafts in Maine. It is disappointing that this progress has not been paralleled in Europe, where the Royal College of Art's glassmaking program is among the few exceptions.

In addition to progress in education, increasing attention has been paid studio artists by museums worldwide. The Toledo Museum extended support with its "Glass Nationals" in 1966, 1968, and 1970 culminating in *American Glass Now* in 1972, jointly sponsored with the Museum of Contemporary Crafts in New York. *Objects: USA,* which opened at the Smithsonian Institution in 1969, included glass in its survey of artist-craftsmen. There have been exhibitions at the Dallas Museum of Fine Arts *(Air, Light, Form: New American Glass,* 1967) and an important European exhibition in Zurich, *Glass Heute: Kunst oder Handwerk?* in 1972. Exhibitions at Frankfurt *(Modernes Glas,* 1976) and Coburg *(Coburger Glaspreis,* 1977), the former including American, European and Asian studio artists, the latter a large show of European glass, are the most recent in this series. *Glass '78* in Japan is a survey of contemporary Japanese glass organized by the Japan Glass Artcrafts Association at the Odakyu Department Store, Tokyo, while exhibitions in America are becoming ever more numerous, including *Glass America, 1978,* sponsored by the Contemporary Art Glass Group and the Glass Art Society; *North Carolina Glass '78,* sponsored by Western Carolina University; and *Fifty Americans in Glass 1978,* presented by the Leigh Yawkey Woodson Art Museum in Wisconsin; there have also been innumerable one-man shows.

The advances since the early sixties have been great. Studio pieces submitted to *New Glass* far outnumbered industrial designs, reversing the situation as recorded in *Glass 1959.* At the same time some of the objects accepted by the jury and submitted by companies were designed by studio artists as unique pieces and as prototypes for or samples of production.

It is in the standardization of basic materials and equipment (which allows makers time to develop ideas and experiment with variations) and the promotion of a more intense interaction between artists, craftsmen, designers, and the industry that the studio movement may have the greatest potential for success. One wonders—will all the resulting activity create the basis for a viable tradition, or will it produce works of so personal a character as to transcend a common style? Probably both. In America, interest in the works of Louis Comfort Tiffany has focused, at times superficially, on his production iridescent ware and lamps, losing sight of the more personal stained or leaded glass windows and their important place in the glassmaking heritage. The recent attention paid to the windows is therefore encouraging; just as glassmakers began to explore abstract forms and innovative materials in the 1950's and 1960's, so too has their awareness of the history of glassmaking developed over the same period.

Geoffrey Beard said of *Glass 1959* that "The fifties closed with this exhibition, in its own way as important to glass designers as the great Paris exhibitions of 1925 and 1937 and the Milan Triennales had been in sorting out some of the future trends....The whole exhibition symbolised a moment in design history, the significance of which is now better understood as the objects can be seen in the context of the emergence of new shapes and improved ideas; the results from good training and experiment. Glass in its contemporary totality has seldom been given a more important showing...."[5] Only time will determine whether *New Glass* documents a beginning or an end.

William Warmus
Assistant Curator
Twentieth-Century Glass
12/7/78

1. Herbert Read, *The Origins of Form in Art,* New York: Horizon Press, 1965, pp. 177-178.
2. Contemporary Art Glass Group, *Glass America, 1978,* New York, 1978, p. 20 (exhibition catalog).
3. Guillaume Janneau, *Modern Glass,* London: The Studio Limited, 1931, p. 13.
4. "Littleton remembers...," *Glass Art,* vol. 4, no. 1, 1976, pp. 20-31, details the early history of this development.
5. Geoffrey Beard, *International Modern Glass,* London: Barrie and Jenkins, 1976, p. 37.

1959-1979

Twenty years ago when five of us met as a jury in a warehouse in Long Island City to make our choices for the exhibition "Glass 1959," we looked at a few more than eighteen hundred entries. From these each of us was asked to select one hundred objects. Those we chose, we were told, would not only appear in the show but in the catalogue, and each piece would carry on its label and caption the initials of the jurors who selected it. The reason for this was to make it quite clear that there were no bargains or compromises in the jury's selections and that five different pairs of eyes with five different and individual standards of taste would be represented. The show might have included five hundred pieces, but taste being what it is and the quality and characteristics of the glass what they were, there was very considerable overlapping in our choices. The same has happened again, twenty years later. This time instead of eighteen hundred pieces the jury (four instead of the earlier five) considered an initial six thousand.

But this is not the same world as the one in which the jury for the 1959 exhibition met. The glass is not the same. The jury's eyes are not the same (I can speak for myself; I am by chance the only repeater from that earlier jury), the condition of the arts and crafts is not the same nor the society for and in which they are created.

Glass is a social art, essentially, an art made for people to use as much as to admire, and as such, much of its character, as I hope to suggest, must vary with social change. (Taste and social change are, of course, interlocked.) The functions of glass range from the most practical and utilitarian—from everyday use as containers of fluid and excluders of weather—to elaborate pieces for the celebration of great occasions, like trophies exchanged by heads of state, or the illumination of ceremonial buildings, like the windows of cathedrals and

the chandeliers of opera houses. The ways in which it is worked vary from contrivances that produce blanks for light bulbs faster than a machine gun produces bullets to the most exquisite and painstaking craftsmanship that employs subtleties of technique with ancient and noble histories. Some of the glass in this exhibition is highly refined utilitarian glass, such as wineglasses and pitchers and bottles; some of it can only be called "art glass" whose function is sensuous, appealing, that is, to the senses of sight and touch. But whether it is utilitarian or made strictly for its own sake as sculpture, the hand and eye of its maker is conditioned by the society or segment of society, however small, which inspires him and which he considers the audience for his virtuosity.

When we judged the glass in the warehouse two decades ago, each piece carefully displayed and lighted for its benefit and ours, we looked at least partly with the eyes of the Bauhaus whose influence, though the school had been closed by the Nazis twenty-five years before, permeated much of what was then regarded as sophisticated taste. We were (in any case I was) the somewhat wayward disciples of functionalism as preached by Walter Gropius and his followers in the United States as well as in Europe. Unnecessary ornament was then regarded as very nearly immoral, straight lines were more godly than curved ones, and if function required curves, as in wineglasses, purity was preferable to playfulness. Not that we adhered to any such doctrine with strictness, but, as our choices looked back on demonstrate, the long shadow of the Bauhaus was there. None of us was primarily a glass expert—an architect, a designer of furniture, the director of a state art museum, a curator of design, and an editor and essayist. We were, however, a small sampling of the context in which the arts of the 1950's were produced. We were all in some degree involved with how our contemporaries looked at what they saw about them, tastemakers in a manner of speaking. The same thing is true of the jury for "New Glass"—an editor of an Italian magazine of design, the director of a New York crafts museum, the director of a German museum of modern art, and the same editor and essayist, twenty years older and, if no wiser, at least subjected to two decades of radical change in the arts and society. This time half the jurors are from Europe. This time there is a woman among us, which in itself says something of social change in the last twenty years.

Years in the near future happen very slowly, one at a time; years in the past, even the immediate past, happen fast—in decades. The attitude toward the arts has changed greatly in the last two decades in America and Europe and in parts of the Orient more greatly, I think, than most of us are aware. Let us look at where we were in 1959, what we have been through since, and how our attitudes have changed. The American experience has, of course, not been duplicated elsewhere, but such are the winds by which the characteristics and attitudes of the arts are disseminated that they have a way of flying over borders and defying the barriers of language.

You may recall that it was in 1957 that the Russians launched the first satellite, Sputnik I, into space, followed soon after by a far larger one carrying a dog. A shocked Western World, not in the least accustomed to being bettered in its scientific and technical accomplishments, decided, in effect, that every able-minded young person should turn his attention to the sciences. This caused a brief educational revolution with results for the benefit of the arts which were not as remote, at least in America, as you might think.

Our educational system was blamed for having given in to the pressures of progressive education which emphasized "self-expression" at the expense of discipline in the "three R's." A result of this was a flood of Federal funds into the educational system in order, it was hoped, to produce a flood of scientists and technologists prepared to compete with the Russians. Many of those who had objected to Federal interference in education, fearing government determination of what should be taught, as is not uncommon in Europe, may not have been silenced, but their voices were muffled with a money gag.

Since the early 1950's there had been a gradual rising tide of support for legislation to provide Federal funds for the arts. Though there was a great expenditure of rhetoric in and out of Congress, it was not until the mid-1960's, partly as a reaction to the stifling of the humanities by the technical and scientific emphasis in education, that the rhetoric elicited a small ooze of Federal funds. It was almost as though the electorate had voted in art when it voted in Kennedy...by a very small margin, to be sure, but a margin nonetheless. Art was no longer a dirty word in the halls of Congress, and artists, who had been looked on as potential if not actual subversives, became national assets, not liabilities. Perversely we can thank Sputnik for some of that. Our over-reaction to it produced a counter-reaction from which the arts and humanities benefitted.

It was during the 1960's that cultural centers blossomed across the country. In 1966, for example, some 300 new arts organizations were given tax-exempt status, and there were more than 100 cultural centers in the planning stages. Lincoln Center in New York was the prototype. Plans for it were initiated in 1955 and ground was broken in 1959, the year of the last international glass exhibition initiated by the Corning Museum of Glass. It was part of a movement to centralize the arts, and it was in some respects inspired by the possibility of getting Federal funds for urban redevelopment, partly for the purpose of saving money by having opera and symphonies, museums and theaters and art schools under a single management, even a single roof. But perhaps more important, such centers were a way to celebrate and publicize the cultural aspirations (some said pretensions) of cities. Each city seemed to want to outdo its counterparts in cultural display. The arts were good for business; they attracted corporations and bright young executive families to communities that could give them "cultural advantages." They also attracted artists delighted to escape the intense competition in the very few art centers of America.

Some of the large cultural plants that blossomed in the 1960's produced at first very small and in many cases pretty tasteless fruits. In some cities like Seattle, whose cultural center was a carefully planned residue of its World's Fair of 1962, the results were salubrious; in Atlanta a few years later they were disappointing. Too much had been spent on construction and too little thought had been given to the programs they were to house and how they could be supported. But be that as it may, the modern ark was amoverin', and local, state and Federal funds were firing its boilers.

If this seems remote from the nature of glass in 1979, bear with me. Glass, as I have said, is a social art and is made not in an aesthetic vacuum but in the context of the other arts and crafts and in the helter-skelter of social accommodations to national and international attitudes and pressures.

Many other factors besides the growth of the art establishment were at work, besides the ambitious cultural centers, the recognition by government of its responsibilities to the arts (and the bureaucracies set up to administer them), the organizations of business groups like the Business Committee for the Arts, and an expanding concern in colleges and universities with fostering the performing arts along with the plastic arts and crafts. Following World War II the population of the United States began to grow at what seemed an alarming rate, and at the same time, as the workweek shrank from forty-eight hours to forty and less, opportunities for leisure vastly increased and with it not only the audience for the arts but the potential participants in them. Museums popped up everywhere and on weekends long lines of people waited for their doors to open. (At the Corning Museum of Glass, for example, some 715,911 visitors came last year from as far as Europe and as near as Elmira, the neighboring city, many to look casually but some to look carefully with delight and to learn.) In the fifties and sixties galleries dealing in art and in the crafts multiplied in large cities like New York and Chicago, Washington and Los Angeles, and appeared in country barns and even deserted churches. Where there had been a few posh art dealers and a few experimental ones, there were now dozens of each and the customers to make them viable.

Add to this another factor. The battle for modern art which began in America with the Armory Show of 1913, where Cubism and Synchronism and Futurism and abstract sculpture first horrified an unready public, had been won. Non-representational art, once anathema, had come to be taken for granted, and it was discovered that abstractions and realism of many sorts could live together congenially, indeed side by side in galleries and museums to shock almost no one. "Modern," which not long ago meant odd and experimental and a revolt from academic tradition, is now regarded as a manifestation which was historically inevitable, a logical step in man's need to explore for the truth and reveal it. From this there emerged not only a new excitement about art but also a tolerance for everything experimental, a belief that "If I don't like it, I ought to try to." At the same time the emphasis in education on "self-expression" and "creativity" (dangerous and muddy clichés when they become a substitute in the arts for discipline and technique) vastly increased the numbers of amateur artists and, at the same time, amateurs of the arts.

In the United States in the 1950's a movement emerged which reversed one of the processes set in motion by the Armory Show. That exhibition to the dismay of American artists had turned the eyes of American collectors away from their native artists to those of Europe, and there was a rush to buy French and German and Italian "modernists" and to ignore the painters and sculptors at home. It was the New York School, also called the Abstract Expressionists and the Action Painters, who turned European eyes to America as the place where the new and exciting and significant was being produced. Jackson Pollock, Robert Motherwell, Willem de Kooning, Mark Rothko, Arshile Gorky and a number of others had picked up the old European challenge of nonfigurative art and given it new dimensions. For the first time in our history American artists were not looking to Europe as the arbiter of taste, the source of innovation, and the standard by which to measure their accomplishments.

The result was a new self-confidence in the American arts which went beyond painting to sculpture and the crafts. The intellectual and creative winds were blowing not just from Europe to our shores but freely in both directions and across the Pacific as well. If American artists gained confidence from this, artists elsewhere lost none. The community of the arts was increasingly knit together by the rapidity of travel—both for artists and works from their hands—and the interchange of ideas became almost instantaneous.

In the sixties, while the official art establishment grew, so did the "counter-culture," the movement especially among the young and in the community of the arts against The Establishment. Along with its political attacks there were attacks on what it regarded as a systematic stifling of individualism. Those who identified themselves with the counter-culture blamed "the system," whether it was exemplified by the corporation or the government or the university, and it was the era of student revolt. It was also a time of quiet revolt during which the crafts movement, which had got its start in the depression years of the 1930's, burgeoned. Many talented young men and women, and some not so talented, turned away from the traditional paths of fulfillment in a money-oriented society to the ideal of shaping their lives by shaping objects with their hands. They turned to paths of artistic endeavor and they explored new uses of old materials and techniques and arrived at new forms and textures as free of academic tradition as the canvases of the Action Painters and the multi-media Conceptualists.

To be sure it was some elements of The Establishment that gave them not only the greatest encouragement but places and means to "do their thing," a phrase of determined individualism that became current in the sixties. It was then that colleges and universities found ways to expand their facilities for the interpretive (i.e., the performing) arts, the fine arts and the crafts as well—for pottery and weaving and metalwork and somewhat later for the making of glass. In hundreds of communities projects were enthusiastically initiated to provide the ways and means for such activities. State arts councils, eager to spread limited funds beyond museums and symphonies and other highly visible and audible institutions, began to allocate a trickle of money to experimental groups in the arts and crafts.

A similar crafts movement, also with government support, has developed in

Great Britain since World War II. In France with its long and distinguished tradition of glassmaking there has been no comparable movement; in Italy, and especially in Murano, the tradition of glass designed by artists and made by artisans in factories persists. In Czechoslovakia artist-designers working with artisans continue to produce glass of the highest quality of design and manufacture. There are many fewer studio glassmakers in Europe that work in the same ways as those in America, though the number increases, especially in Sweden, but the studio tradition in the making of stained glass is enjoying new energy and exploring new methods and concepts. But if distinctions of method can be drawn, distinctions of inspiration are elusive.

As Thomas Buechner wrote of a glass exhibition in Coburg in 1977 (it included glass from seventeen European nations), "Too many people are doing too many different things to be regarded as esoteric and inconsequential aberrations. Glass has become a medium of personal expression. Surprisingly the variety of work seemed to transcend any suggestion of national style....Part of the great change appears to be the dissolution of groupings of compatriots who, consciously or not, adhered to some common taste or aesthetic notion." This suggests, as the current exhibition also suggests, the emergence of a new "international style," not like the one of the 1930's in architecture promulgated by the Bauhaus or the one of the fourteenth century in painting except in its confounding of national characteristics and its acceptance of individual style.

As is explained in detail elsewhere in this catalogue, by far the greater proportion of exhibits are craftsmen's glass. In the 1959 exhibition about ninety per cent of the glass was "factory glass" and ten per cent glass conceived and made by craftsmen working as individual artists. This time the percentages are almost reversed and so are the intentions of their makers. Functional glass (or

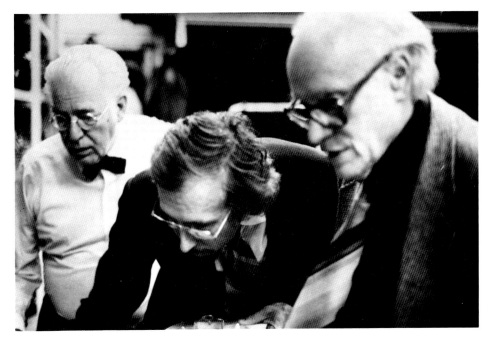

utilitarian glass no matter how refined and beautifully designed and executed) in this exhibition is largely the production of factories, and the sculptural glass is the work of craftsmen. The products of twenty-eight countries are represented in the collection which, I believe, speaks for the universality of excellence in design and craftsmanship but also for the catholicity of the jurors' tastes. In general we did not know, when we made our selections, which pieces were made in what places or by what artists.

As I look again after a good many years at the catalog of "Glass 1959," I see in it a very different world from today. Things seem to have been tidier, more self-contained, understated, orderly and polite than in the society suggested by "New Glass." By contrast the new glass is more romantic and flowing on the one hand and expressionist and tough on the other, freer in its design, more explosive. Its costume is blue jeans not black-tie, unmoved by the forms of etiquette and the manners of formality which pervaded the glass of 1959. It is often ebullient both in shape and intention and in sheer size and weight. It is more insistent and brash and demanding. Some of it speaks with a new humor (sometimes black humor) and some of it is satirical. Whimsy has less to do with it than the glass of twenty years ago, and fantasy has more. The influence of sci-fi?

Much of the new glass seems to me more personal and introverted than the old, more determined to bear the stamp of individuality, to serve private not public satisfactions—"in" glass for the inner man. Above all it is more experimental and determined to employ old materials and techniques and by combining them in new ways with new materials to force them into fresh dimensions of expression one can only applaud. But it is not all of that sort.

Through this exhibition runs a parallel strain of traditional response and compliance to man's needs and gratifications in a medium of expression that is as demanding of an artist's skill as it is submissive to his imagination. However great the differences in "Glass 1959" and "New Glass" they share the qualities of demand and delight with the glass that was shaped by ancient glassmakers 2,000 years ago.

Russell Lynes
New York City

Jury Statements

Franca Santi Gualteri

When I agreed to be on this jury, I knew I had no specific knowledge of the art of glassmaking, so I cannot now start to criticize the various items displayed. I can tell you, though, how I felt about the task, and how I made my choices.

At the beginning I had to sort through 6,000 color slides. My initial reaction to this bombardment was to make a mental—and instinctive—division of all the objects into four broad categories: functional things (like glasses, table and kitchen ware); stained glass; decorative things (like vases, bowls, and such); sculptures.

The first objects I "saw," naturally, were the items in the first group. I say "naturally," because it is a normal part of my job to think about household equipment as part of the home as a whole. In this category I had no difficulty dividing the "goodies" from the "badies," establishing which items were well designed, and discarding those which looked wrong because they were too much like remnants of the past, or because their approach to the "modern line" was wrong.

The first things I excluded were the stained glass and glass panels with leading. This I did as a matter of principle, even though their transparency was often captivating, because I felt they were all out of place in today's home—like reproduction furniture, they somehow didn't feel right. It was harder for me to decide in the last two groups. My idea was to try to establish a rational motivation for saying yes or no, but strangely enough this soon gave way to a definite feeling of certainty: I found I was grouping things as material objects and color subjects. Among the former, I looked for the least "redundant" items, the purest as regards geometry and volume; among the latter I tried to find articles whose color was an integral part of the glass, and whose decorative elements were light enough not to overwhelm the whole piece. When I saw the actual items, though, all these carefully calculated divisions, groupings, and criteria evaporated or were upturned because the photos were always influenced not only by the photographer's ability but also by his interpretation. Many of the household items I had selected for their straightforward lines turned out "in the flesh" to be too flat and lifeless, with no novelty or imagination.

In contrast, all my "rationale" went to pieces when, faced with the splendor of glass, I ended up choosing complicated sculptures—not just redundant, but totally overdone! Fascinated by the manual skill of whoever had actually produced these impossible articles, I ended up choosing useless, sophisticated objects which I found beautiful! My preference, though, went to a few small things—a white bowl with two pink brush-marks, big and small bottles with fancy tops, impractical chalices with a tiny bowl and stork-like legs—full of poetry and a touch of humor, qualities some of the bigger, most beautiful things often didn't manage to achieve.

To conclude, one note of regret—too few Italians took part in this competition. This was a pity for several reasons—for example, if you think about Ettore

Sottsass Jr.'s vases for Vistosi, his use of material and color, with tremendous inventiveness, would have reaffirmed the Murano glassworking tradition and provided proof of its vitality and ability to rejuvenate itself.—F.S.G.

Franca Santi Gualteri *is editor of* Abitare, *the important Italian design magazine, a position she has held since 1974. She created the publication "Mettiamo su Casa Insieme," which is presently published as an insert for* Abitare, *in 1971. Mrs. Santi has been a free-lance journalist and from 1953 until 1963 was on the editorial staff of* Stile Industria. *She holds a degree (1951) from the Brera Academy of Fine Arts in Milano, Italy.*

Russell Lynes

Consider a room a little smaller than half a tennis court from net to baseline and from alley to alley. Down one wall is a row of raw wooden shelves, down the other a row of trestle tables, and across the width are half a dozen stacks of shelves a yard or so apart. The stacks and the tables are covered with hundreds of objects of glass, nearly a thousand in fact. They are quiet, self-contained, and as alive as light through them and bounced off their surface can make them. You walk past them very slowly, pausing frequently. Each object, no matter how small, seems to say, "choose me," and each has its very special bold or delicate reason for insisting it should be chosen. The larger pieces, sculpture of a spacial sort with only a single common ingredient, glass, too big for shelves, are on the tables and in two adjoining rooms (one darkened to give illuminated objects their due) where they can be walked around. You can pick up the smaller objects, turn them in your hands, hold them up to brighter light than falls on the shelves. Later you will look at them on light tables or under spotlights. Each is given every chance. Size, you quickly decide, does not matter...though scale in proportion to use or to intention matters essentially.

I have been asked to put down briefly my criteria for selecting pieces for this exhibition. I began with no preconceived criteria. Judging such objects in such circumstances is a matter of making comparisons, not an excercise in rigid absolutes. In my case my criteria emerged as I looked, which means that they were essentially subjective. I started not with a comprehensive knowledge of glass but with an eye long practiced in making visual judgments. One does not judge glass as one judges stone or paint on canvas or textiles, but one uses the same accumulation of visual experience, the same pleasure in the practice of optical taste, and, one hopes, the same openness to new experience.

Originality? Yes and no. Originality that strains for the effect of being original is like a too loud voice in a quiet room. It is arrogant without being individual, show without substance. It is not hard to distinguish the kind of originality that is striven for for its own sake and the kind that evolves out of an artist's individual efforts to achieve a personal statement. A nineteenth century writer put it this way: "Originality does not consist in saying what no one has ever said before, but in saying exactly what you think yourself." Some of the glass had that kind of originality. It was easy to spot.

Quality? It is a criterion as many-faceted as glass. Quality of craftsmanship, quality of intellect, quality of inspiration, quality of design and appropriateness, quality of material. Quality of material matters in glass as quality of stones in jewelry or threads in embroidery and has its own tactile and visual delights, but though it is an important means it is not an end, and as in any work of art it is the end that matters. I have always been put off by the proposition that one should understand what an artist is "trying to do." It is not the "trying" that matters to the artist or to me; it is the result that matters. The quality of the material may be breathtaking, the technique pure wizardry, and the result a bore. The history of the arts and crafts is filled with such exquisite failures. I tried to pick the successes.

So much for the criteria. The impressive thing about what we were given to judge was the range of inspirations, the variety of the ends achieved, the generally high quality of craftsmanship, the sensitiveness of imagination, and the freedom with which an untouchable material (molten glass) was worked with individuality. It was endowed with qualities beyond its natural state to satisfy in hand and mind and eye what seemed to my perhaps peculiar but certainly particular vision the satisfying quality of delight.—R.L.

Russell Lynes *is presently a columnist for the* Architectural Digest *and is the author of innumerable publications; his books include* Highbrow, Lowbrow, Middlebrow, The Taste-makers, A Surfeit of Honey, The Domesticated Americans, *and* Confessions of a Dilettante. *From 1944-1968 he was an editor of* Harper's Magazine. *Mr. Lynes is a former president of the Archives of American Art and a member of the Visiting Committee for American Art at The Metropolitan Museum of Art.*

Werner Schmalenbach

The organizers of this competition took a risk when they stated that they intended to have not only "glass people" but "art people" on the Jury—a circumstance that, among other things, explains why I had the pleasure of being asked to serve. The advantage of a certain distance and impartiality that was probably anticipated from this idea was balanced by the substantial risk that the Jury, at least in part, would be lacking in expertise. I won't deny that I accepted with some misgivings; for how was I, someone who had been involved all his life with the visual arts and hardly at all with glass, to pass judgment in a field in which I possess little, if any, knowledge. Then I said to myself: the organizers want it that way, they want to take this risk, and so I said that I was ready to serve, troubled only by the fact that we would have to judge thousands of glasses, first from their slides and then the originals.

To my surprise, my powers of judgment functioned in the most matter-of-fact way and almost automatically, which did not preclude occasional uncertainties, errors, and subsequent corrections. While the slides went by in rapid succession, I felt like a thermometer whose column of mercury immediately and almost involuntarily rose or fell at the sight of each glass, coming to rest at a quite precise place on the scale, in the "yes"-area or the "no"-area depending on the individual case. The "yes" and "no" were recorded with a corresponding speed. I'll leave it to others to ponder over the relative subjectivity or relative objectivity of such decisions.

A further personal confession: after the initial viewing of all the works, I had selected hundreds of glasses that were still "in the running." There were not only many too many, but also substantially more than those of my colleagues on the Jury; we—all independently of each other—had to judge the same slides. Then, however, on the second viewing, the opposite occurred, and I had substantially fewer pieces left than the others. I think that made very good sense: the first time through I behaved magnanimously, took my time, wanted to see this or that work again, and in this way let my standards for judging develop on the basis of the objects; you might say that I followed the legal principle *in dubio pro reo* (give the defendant the benefit of the doubt). On the second viewing my tolerance was transformed into intolerance: now doubt was an argument against the "defendant"; the standard had become clear and confirmed; in place of relaxed friendliness and limited responsibility there was now the far less relaxed severity of responsible judgment.

In addition, there were further possibilities for correction: the subsequent joint judging of all the selected slides and then, some months later, the final judging of the originals. When we were confronted with the originals, many things seemed quite different: the size, the colors, the light, the space, in other words, essential elements in making a judgment. Although this made it clear that we might have done some works an injustice on the basis of the slides, still the process as a whole proved to be optimal; there is no such thing as an ideal process.

Don't ask me for the criteria I used in making my choice! Such criteria are in any case questionable as a matter of principle, and can hardly be made objective, can hardly be rationalized. In this undertaking, the criteria were particularly open to doubt, since the offerings extended from simple household glasses to highly decorative glass sculptures. In the first case, it is not merely the visual impression that is important but also the fulfillment of a useful function, which is lacking in the second case. Besides, the most cheerful pluralism of style held sway: primitivisms and archaisms on the one hand; on the other hand, extreme refinement, with both being equally capable of merit and weakness. There are extremely geometrical, cubic objects in which a severe, as it were, ideological spirit is present; and there are playful, even humorous creations that are often particularly compatible with the fluid nature of glass. Pure form, playful fantasy, humor, even pathos; all possibilities are represented.

Even a work that contradicts the nature of glass can be outstanding once in a while on the basis of its inventiveness. If a person starts from fixed criteria in making such a selection, then there is the risk that he is not judging freely but on the basis of a preconception. In the proceedings of the Jury it was plainly apparent that none of us was fixed in any direction, but that each made his personal choice and perhaps now and then also committed his personal error.

To someone like me, whose background is art, the role of "taste" in such a task is an intriguing subject. In the field of art we have long been distrustful of taste, since we expect something quite different from the expression of taste to be operative in art. Obviously, then, there are significant differences between the products of the artist and, for example, those of the glassmaker. For in the field of glass, ceramics, textiles, etc., taste—both as a criterion of manufacture and a criterion of evaluation—plays a larger and more important role. People have been wanting for almost a century now to bridge the gap between fine art and craftsmanship, but this is wishful thinking unless we have the wisdom to view this desire with detachment and accept the fact that these are two fundamentally separate fields, even when, as may happen now and then, the gap is bridged, perhaps by an artist, perhaps by a craftsman in glass. The exceptions prove a rule that is really not at all objectionable. It is nonsensical to want to bring the "art" of glass unconditionally into the field of fine art, but it is beyond doubt that in the works of the glassmaker—the exhibit proves this—there is often more artistic genius at work than in many works of painting or sculpture. Therefore we ought indeed to keep the categories separate, but not rank them hierarchically above one another; we should not mix them together but search in each of the separate fields for the traces and forms of artistic sensibility. It was the task of the Jury to do this in the field of glass.—W.S.

Werner Schmalenbach *has assembled one of Europe's most important collections of modern and contemporary art at the Museum für Moderne Kunst, Düsseldorf, West Germany, where he is Director. His numerous exhibitions include the first full scale retrospective of the work of Kurt Schwitters (1956). Among his publications are works about Fernand Léger and Schwitters and studies of African art and the film.*

Paul J. Smith

It has been an impressive experience to see the energy, imagination, and skill in the broad range of work submitted for *New Glass.* Considering its history of almost 4,000 years, glass as a medium today still remains an exciting challenge to the creative artist, designer, and industry. During the last twenty years we have seen a new glass technology become vital to the space program and scientific research. In contrast, we have in the same period witnessed the expansion of the Studio Movement in which the artists working directly in glass use the simplest traditional methods of free-blown and constructed techniques. This movement has developed a new glass aesthetic which, as a reflection of our time, blends the past with the present.

Characteristic of modern glass now is an international style, the result of worldwide communication among artists and designers. By means of publications, conferences, workshops, and international exhibitions, the glass artists share information and are in turn inspired by each other's work. With global interchange the national image is obviously disappearing; however, replacing it is the artist drawing upon his or her heritage yet working in individualistic patterns.

As I made my selections for the exhibition it became obvious that the entries basically divided into three groups—functional ware designed for production, objects designed by artists and executed by artisans, and the object designed and made solely by the artist. In this latter group, with its full range of container forms and sculptural statements, the work was the most exciting. It demonstrated the greatest development through experimentation while using many traditional techniques—cutting, etching, molding, laminating—and in sculptural pieces employing materials such as wood, metal, plastic, sand, and neon. The most disappointing area was the production ware which for the most part had little sense of originality. My choices for the *New Glass* exhibition have been concerned with sensitive personal statements, ideas which manifest the love of the material and process, and with objects which have something to say whether sculptural, utilitarian, one-of-a-kind or mass produced. I salute the artists in this exhibition who have united history with the present and have contributed works of beauty in the ageless substance of glass.—P.J.S.

Paul J. Smith *lives in New York City where he is Director of the Museum of Contemporary Crafts of the American Crafts Council. Mr. Smith is known internationally as a juror, lecturer, and consultant on contemporary crafts and design, and is a painter and craftsman who has exhibited works in metal, wood, and ceramics. He attended the Art Institute of Buffalo and the School for American Craftsmen in Rochester, New York. Paul J. Smith is active on the boards of several organizations and is Vice-President of The Louis Comfort Tiffany Foundation.*

Catalog of the Exhibition

The initials of the judges are listed below the captions of the objects they chose. Every entrant is represented by a color plate. If the entrant has more than one entry, subsequent plates are in black and white. Dimensions are abbreviated: H. (Height); D. (Diameter); W. (Width).

1
Heads of Men
H. 21.3 cm, D. (max) 34.8 cm
Date: February 1978
Signature: JAN ADAM 78
Colorless glass, mold-blown.
Enameled.

RL, PS

◄2
Head
H. (with Base) 32.6 cm,
W. 25.5 cm
Date: November 1977
Signature: ADENSAMOVA
Colorless glass, blown in plaster
mold. Enameled. Engraved and
sandblasted.

RL, PS

3
Pear
H. 23.7 cm, D. 15.9 cm
Date: Made January 1976;
designed April 1974
Signature: Anchor Hocking Con-
temporary Crystal (on paper
label)
Designer: J. Lloyd Thrush
Colorless glass. Produced on
automatic blowing machine.
Pressed cover.

WS

4
Apple
H. 16.9 cm, D. 17.7 cm
Description same as Pear, 3.

Armbruster
United States

5
Wandering Matter One
H. 23 cm, W. 91 cm, Depth 91 cm.
Date: February 10, 1978
Signature: T W Armbruster
Sheet glass and colorless glass,
blown. Sandblasted. Sand.

FS-G, RL, WS, PS

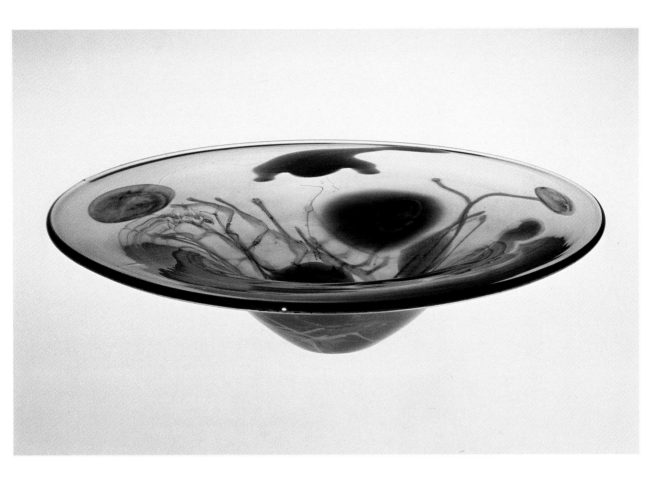

6
Image Bowl. *Passage*
H. 9.1 cm, D. 38.5 cm
Date: 1977
Signature: Herbert Babcock '1977'
Copper-red tinted glass, blown.
Colored bits applied hot and
worked with tools.

RL

Compagnie des Cristalleries de Baccarat
France

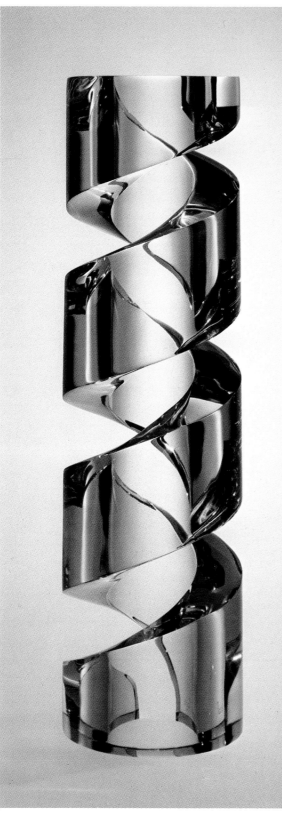

7
VIS
H. 40 cm, D. 12 cm
Date: Made 1978; designed 1978
Signature: Baccarat
Edition: 1/100
Colorless glass, blown. Cut.

RL, WS

8 a-d
Angle
H. (tallest) 23.4 cm, W. 14.7 cm
Date: Made 1977; designed 1977
Signature: Baccarat/Sambonet/
trademark
Designer: Sambonet
Colorless glass, mold-blown. Cut.

PS

9 a-c
Wooly Eggs
H. (tallest) 37.1 cm, D. 31.5 cm
Date: March 1977
Signature: Monica Backström
BODA 76 SWEDEN-MB 261 1400
Company: Kosta Boda AB
Colorless glass, blown. Spun glass
threads inside two eggs only.

FS-G, RL, WS, PS

Bāncilá
Romania

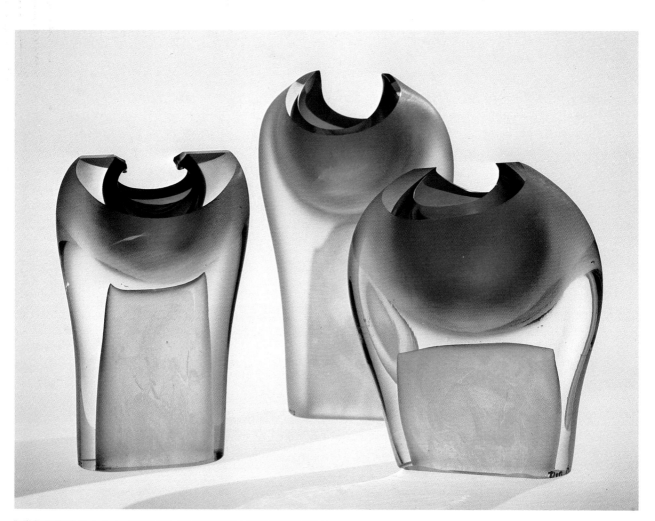

10 a-c
Blue Shapes
H. (tallest) 24.5 cm, W. 14.8 cm
Date: January-February 1978
Signature: Dan Bāncilá 1978
Blue and white glass, blown. Cut
and acid-etched.

FS-G, RL, WS, PS

11 a-d
Genesys I
H. (tallest) 66.2 cm
Date: January-February 1978
Signature: D. B 1978
Green glass, blown. Acid-etched.

PS

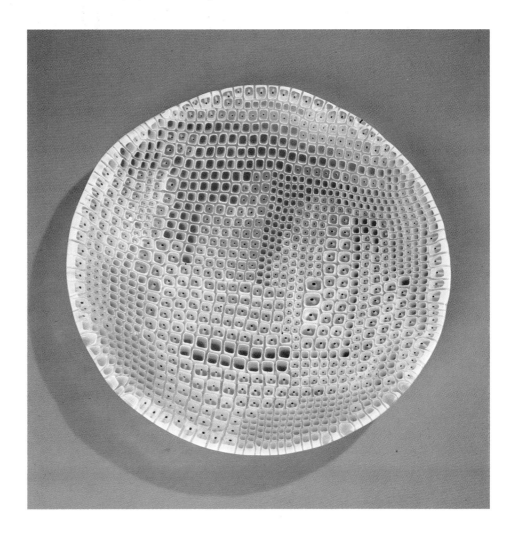

12
Bowl *Murrine*
H. 7.3 cm, D. 46 cm
Date: 1976
Signature: F.A. Barbini
Gray and white glass canes
arranged in irregular patterns,
fused.

RL, PS

Bartron
United States (working in Sweden)

13
Brown Bottle with
Tree Stopper
H. 23.9 cm, W. 10.3 cm,
Depth 8.5 cm
Date: Spring 1978
Signature: Paula Bartron/1978
Colorless glass, blown-molded.
Colored glass decoration.

FS-G, RL, WS, PS

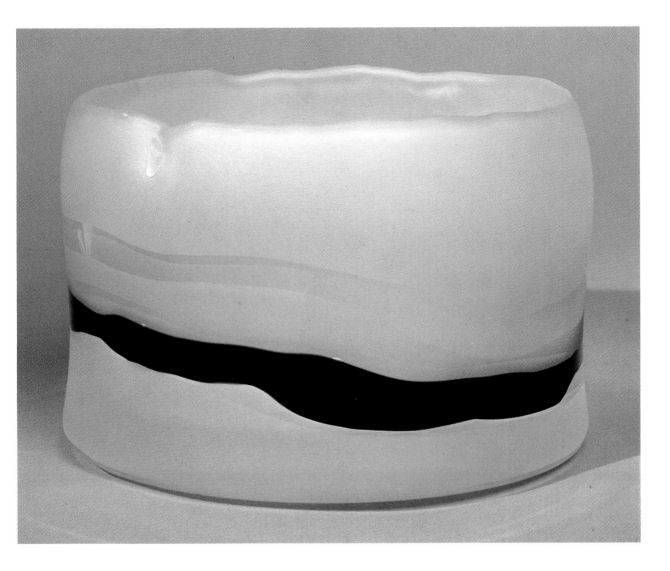

14
Vase
H. 14.6 cm, D. 22.6 cm
Date: June 1977
Signature: 1/6.77/Süssmuth/
Baumann
Company: Süssmuth Gmbh,
Glashütte
Colorless glass, blown. Black
horizontal ribbon decoration.
Acid-etched.

RL

Baumann
Federal Republic of Germany

15
Vase
H. 25.4 cm, W. 23.2 cm,
Depth 12 cm
Date: June 1977
Signature: SÜSSMUTH/
BAUMANN; 016/77
Company: Süssmuth Gmbh,
Glashütte
Colorless glass, blown. Black
glass threads through body.
Acid-etched.

FS-G

16
Bottle
H. 31.1 cm, D. 12.1 cm
Date: August 1977
Signature: 3/8/77/Süss-
muth/S/Baumann
Company: Süssmuth Gmbh,
Glashütte
Colorless glass, blown. Black rib-
bon decoration. Acid-etched.

RL

48

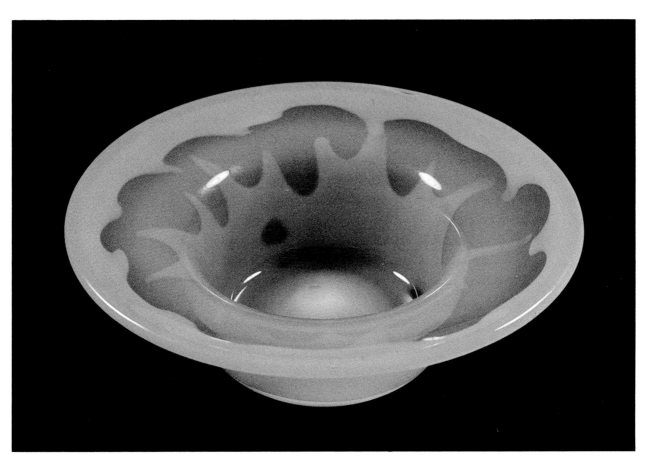

17
Bowl
H. (approx.) 8 cm
Date: March 1977
Colorless glass encasing white
opalescent glass, blown.
Artist's slide.
Object delayed in transit.

FS-G, WS

Ben Tré
United States

18
Burial Box: Type II-Rose
H. 9.9 cm, W. 13.4 cm,
Depth 11.5 cm
Date: February 1978
Signature: BEN TRÉ/2/78
Amber tinted glass, cast.

RL, PS

19
Stonehenge; Series: III
H. 19.2 cm, D. 13.4 cm
Date: August 1977
Signature: PILCHUCK 77/BEN TRÉ
Colorless and pink tinted glass
with colored glass decoration,
blown.

RL

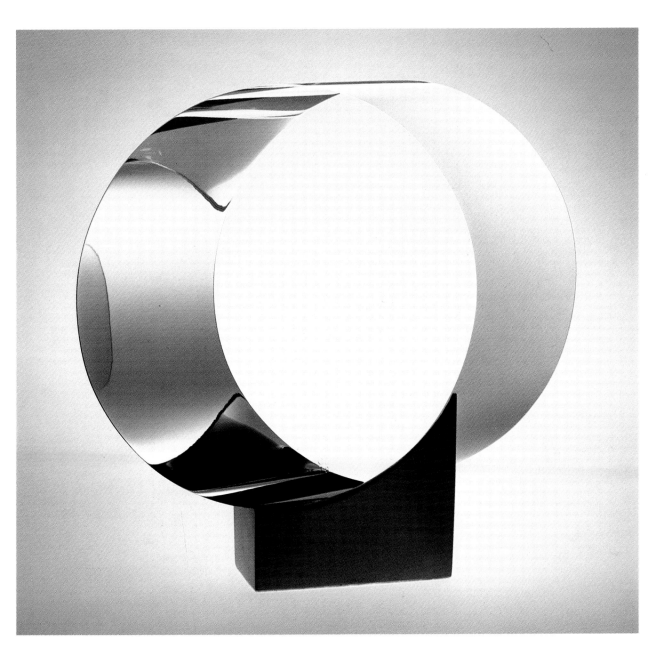

20
Untitled
H. (with base) 26.3 cm, W. 31 cm
Date: March 1978
Signature: cb/78
Colorless optical quality glass,
cast. Polished.

FS-G, RL, WS, PS

21
Cow on a Hill Think'n
Sweet Thoughts
H. 21.7 cm, D. 16.6 cm
Date: March 1978
Signature: RICKY BERNSTEIN 78
Opalescent glass with applied
colored glass decoration. Cased
with colorless glass. Blown.

FS-G, RL, WS, PS

22
Reflection #3
H. 11.3 cm, D. 8.5 cm
Date: 1978
Signature: Bernst/1978
Colorless glass with colored glass
decoration, blown.

FS-G, RL, WS, PS

23
Reflection #1
H. 14.3 cm, D. 8.4 cm
Date: 1978
Signature: Bernst/1978
Colorless glass with colored glass
decoration, blown.

RL, WS, PS

Betz-Schlierer
Federal Republic of Germany

24
Sparkling Star
Approx. 65x72x20 cm
Date: 1977
Plate glass. Cut and cemented.

WS

25
Cathedral II
Approx. 40x45x45 cm
Date: 1977
Plate glass. Cut and cemented.
Mirrored base.

WS

*Artist's slide. Object broken in
transit; not shown in exhibition.*

26 a-d
Cups
H. (tallest) 8.9 cm, W. 16.6 cm
Date: March 1978
Signature: Jonathan Block/Bell-
ingham/1978
Edition: 1/1
Black glass, blown. Fumed irides-
cent surface. Cut and polished.

PS

Bohus
Hungary

27
Space Spiral II
H. 13.5 cm, D. 30.8 cm
Date: 1977
Green tinted glass, laminated and
cut. Three separate elements.

RL, PS

28 | 29
| 30

28 a-c
Ann
H. (tallest) 24.4 cm, D. 3.9 cm
Date: 1977
Signature: Handmade/Boda/
Sweden (on paper label)
Company: Kosta Boda AB
Colorless glass, blown.

FS-G, RL

29 a-c
Marie
H. (tallest) 23.4 cm, D. 6.8 cm
Date: 1977
Signature: Handmade/Boda/
Sweden (on paper label)
Company: Kosta Boda AB
Colorless glass, blown.

WS

30
Boda White Wine *Roemer*
H. 5.3 cm, D. 7.7 cm
Date: 1977
Signature: Handmade/Boda/
Sweden (on paper label)
Company: Kosta Boda AB
Colorless glass, blown.

FS-G, RL

Burton
United States

31
Sherry
H. 11.2 cm, D. 4.7 cm
Date: 1976
Signature: a/John Burton/
Original (on paper label);
Colorless glass. Lampwork.

FS-G

32
Small Bottle
H. 16.5 cm, D. 13.2 cm
Date: March 1978
Signature: Cá d'oro
1978/designer M Seguso
Designer: Mario Seguso
Gray-amber tinted glass, mold-
blown.

RL, PS

Castellan
United States

33
Striped Bowl
H. 21.7 cm, D. 19.3 cm
Date: March 1978
Signature: D. CASTELLAN/3/78
Colorless glass enclosing opaque
white threads, blown.

RL

34a-e ▶
Tabac 222 Group
H. (largest) 19.2 cm
Date: 1977
Signature: Chihuly/77
Opalescent tan and gray glass,
blown. Some with trailed colored
decoration, some with metallic
surfaces.

RL, PS

Chihuly
United States

35
Star Bayeta
H. 30.5 cm, D. 13.8 cm
Date: 1976
Colored glass, blown. Marvered
lampwork decoration. Iridescent
surface.

RL, PS

36
A Basin Full of
Stars and Stripes!
H. 16 cm, D. 21 cm
Date: June 1976
Signature: Dillon/4776
Colorless glass with colored
stripe decoration. Cased with opal-
escent white glass, blown.

RL

Clarke, J.
United States

37
Father and Son Goblet
H. 36.2 cm, W. 15 cm, D. 9.8 cm
Date: April 1976
Signature: James P. Clarke
Amethyst glass, blown. Acid-etched.

PS

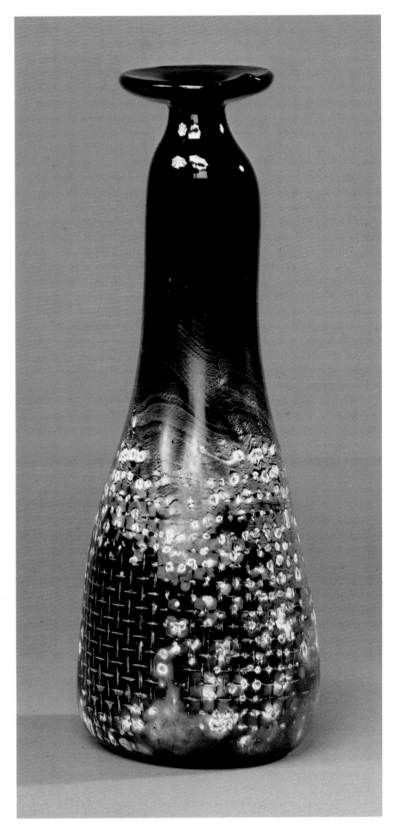

38
Snow Country
H. 31 cm, D. 11.8 cm
Date: May 1976
Signature: R. Cmarik '76
Black glass, blown. Texture
applied by a galvanized wire
mesh form.

RL

Cohn
United States

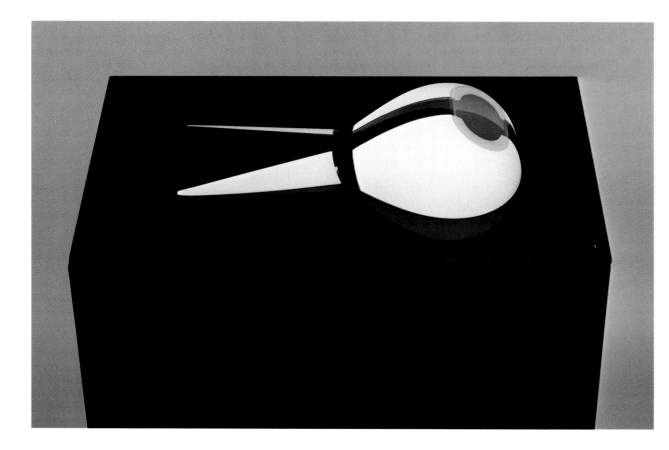

39
Black Plate #3
H. (with base) 110 cm, W. 26 cm,
D. 50.5 cm
Date: 1976
Signature: BP03/Cohn 1977
Opaque white and gray tinted
glass, blown. Cut. One part with
blue reflecting film. Fabricated.
On glass baseplate; black formica
pedestal.

PS

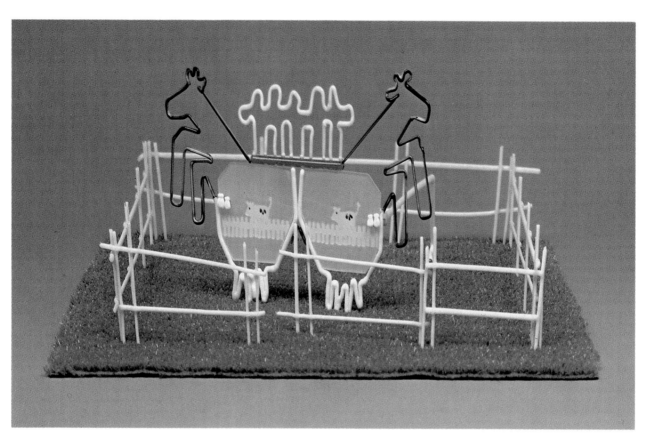

40
Ricky Cow Catchers
H. (of glasses) 13.8 cm,
W. 23.3 cm, Depth 21.2 cm
Date: December 1977
Colored glass. Lampwork.
Slumped, sandblasted, assembled
cold. Plastic turf.

PS

Cook
United Kingdom
England

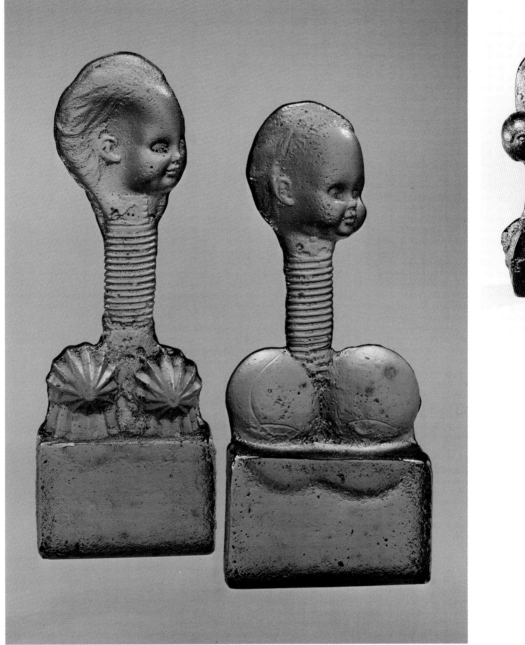

41
Long Neck Clear
H. 31.9 cm, W. 12.1 cm,
Depth 6.5 cm
Date: November 1977
Signature: John Cook 1977
Colorless glass, sand-cast.

PS

68

42
Long Neck Clear
H. 28.9 cm, W. 13 cm,
Depth 6.4 cm
Date: November 1977
Signature: John Cook 77
Colorless glass, sand-cast.

WS

43
Purple Lady
H. 23.6 cm, W. 11.1 cm
Date: November 1977
Signature: John Cook 1977
Amethyst glass, sand-cast.

WS, PS

44
Sherry Glass
H. 13.1 cm, D. 6.8 cm.
Date: Made June 11, 1977;
designed June 6, 1977
Signature: Cowdy Glass
Workshop
Designer: Annette Meech
Colorless glass with bands of
applied colored glass, blown.

FS-G

45
Bowl B 927-77
H. 25.4 cm, D. 30.6 cm
Date: 1977
Signature: ORREFORS/Graal B
927-77/Gunnar Cyrén
Company: AB Orrefors Glasbruk
"Graal" technique, blown.

FS-G

46
Bowl B 1166-78
H. 14.8 cm, D. 23.7 cm
Date: January 1978
Signature: Orrefors Expo B 1166-
78 Gunnar Cyrén
Company: AB Orrefors Glasbruk
Colorless glass, blown. Cut and
acid-etched.

FS-G, PS

47
Cedar Grove Motif Vase
H. 31.9 cm, D. 19.2 cm
Date: July 1977
Signature: S-2 1977; Dailey
Edition: S-2-77/11
Pale blue tinted glass, blown.
Sandblasted.

FS-G, WS, PS

Daum & Cie
France

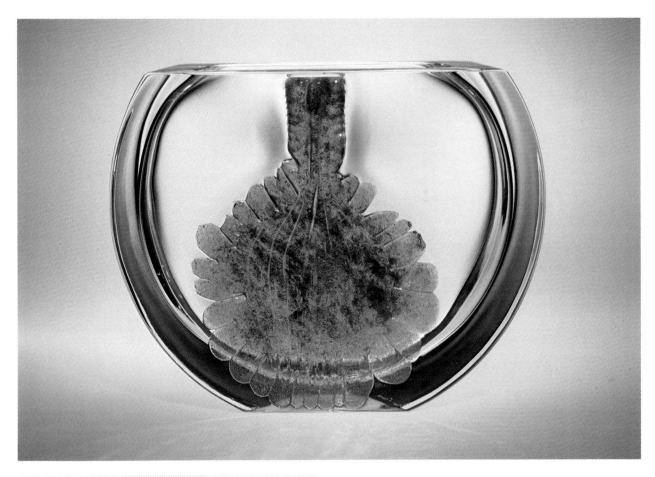

48
Cluny 33
H. 16.1 cm, W. 21.9 cm
Date: Designed January 1978
Signature: Daum France;
CRISTAL/DAUM (on paper label)
Colorless glass with pâte-de-verre
ornament, mold-blown.

FS-G, WS

49 a-c
Corail
H. (tallest) 21.5 cm, D. 5.9 cm
Date: 1977
Signature: Daum France;
CRISTAL/DAUM
(on paper label)
Colorless glass, blown. Hand
applied stem.

FS-G, RL, WS

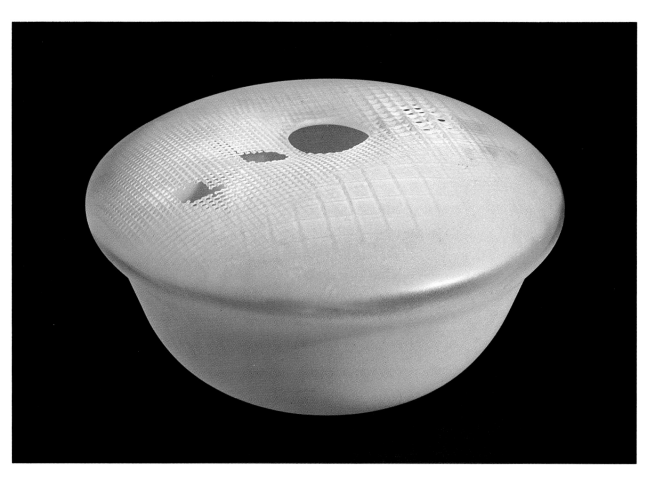

50
Lattice 3
H. 11.6 cm, D. 25.3 cm
Date: January/February 1978
Signature: DEXTER 78
Edition: 3/40
Colorless glass, blown. Sand-
blasted.

FS-G, RL, PS

51 a-c
Pairs
H. 17.3 cm, W. 13.2 cm
Date: January 1977
Colorless glass. Cut and polished.
Object rests on mirror.

RL, WS

52
Reflective Object # 1
H. 11.9 cm, W. 13.7 cm
Date: January 1977
Colorless glass. Cut and polished.

FS-G, RL, WS, PS

53
Ado II
H. 17.7 cm, W. 12 cm,
Depth 9 cm
Date: February 1978
Signature: ANTONIN DROBNÍK
1978
Pale-blue tinted glass,
blown-molded. Applied molded
decoration.

FS-G

Duggan
United States

54
Olympia
H. (approx.) 35 cm, W. 35 cm,
Depth 30 cm
Date: May 1976
Flat glass. Sandblasted, cut,
ground, drilled and cemented.
With neon.

PS

*Artist's slide. Object broken in
transit; not shown in exhibition.*

55
Vase
H. 15.8 cm, D. 13.9 cm
Date: January 1978
Signature: Edelmann/78
Colorless glass with metal inclusions, blown.

RL

Eisch, E.
Federal Republic of Germany

a

Hope is a rope

b

c

d

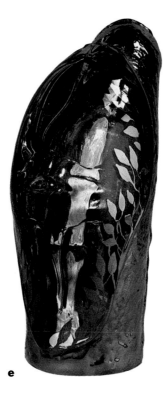

e

56 a-e
Fingers' Studies
a– Finger's Womb
b– Finger's Thought
c– Finger's Love
d– Finger's Pain
e– Finger's Tomb
H. (of a) 45.1 cm, D. 16.6 cm
Date: 1978 (a-e)
Signature: E. Eisch 78
Colorless glass, blown in clay
mold. Enameled and silvered.

PS

57
Overboiled Dream
H. 29.7 cm, W. 16.5 cm
Date: 1978
Signature: G. Eisch 78
Colorless glass blown in clay
mold. Enameled and silvered.

RL

Esson
United Kingdom
England (working in Australia)

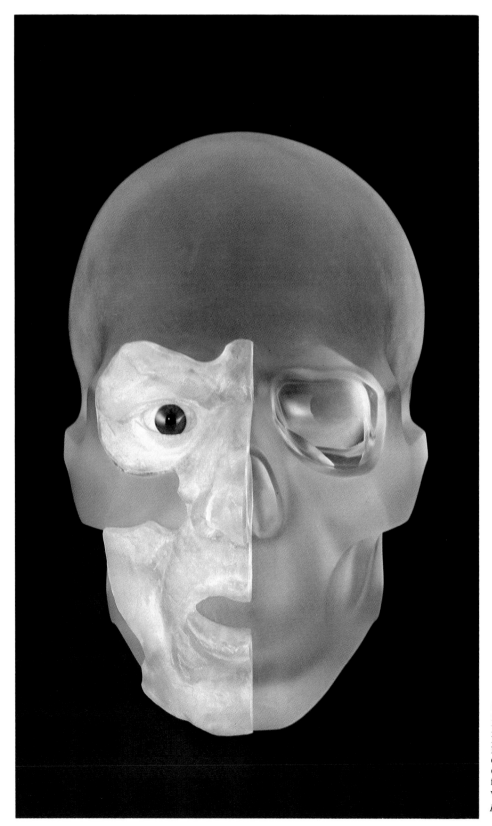

58
Self Portrait
H. 17.9 cm, W. 15.8 cm,
Depth 26.2 cm
Date: Completed June, 1977
Colorless glass, optical quality.
Cast and cut. Cast and cemented
form enclosing lampwork eye;
with hologram.

FS-G, RL, WS, PS

59
Dream Fantasy
H. 19.5 cm, D. 21.6 cm
Date: Completed March 1978
Signature: Ray Flavell/1978
Colorless lead glass, blown. Sand-
blasted decoration.

FS-G, WS

Forsell
Sweden

60
Castle in the Air
H. (tallest form) 66.3 cm,
D. 12.4 cm
Date: February 1978
Signature: ULLA FORSELL/1978
Blown and cast glass; colors
applied by casing and trailing.

RL, PS

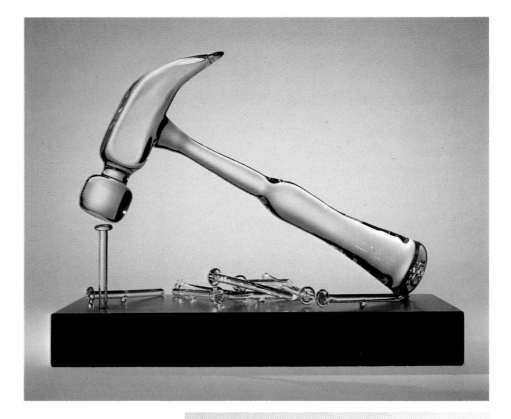

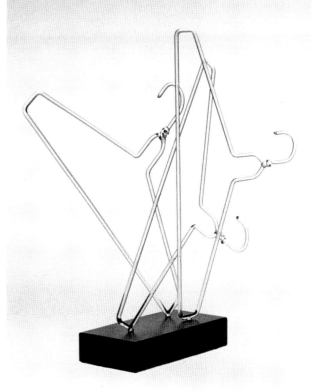

61
Hammer
H. 23.6 cm, L. (hammer) 28.8 cm
Date: 1977
Signature: GF; 1978
Colorless glass. Lampwork.

FS-G, RL, WS

62
Hangers
H. 45.5 cm
Date: 1977
Signature: GF/1978
Colorless glass. Lampwork.

RL, WS, PS

Funakoshi
Japan

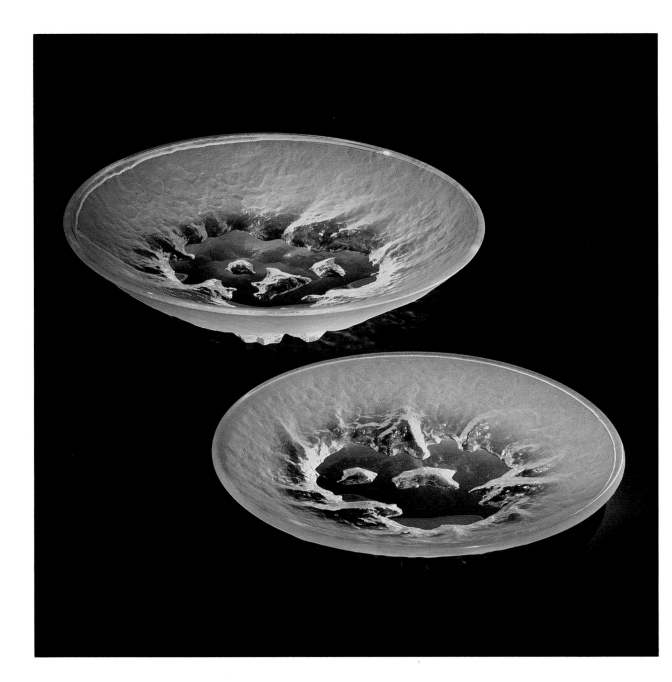

63 a-b
Crystal Dish (2 sizes)
D. (largest) 30.2 cm
Date: January 1976
Company: Hoya Corporation
Colorless glass, hand-pressed.
Sandblasted decoration.

FS-G, RL, PS

64
Untitled
H. 49.9 cm, W. 68.1 cm
Date: March 1977
Colorless, red, and white flat glass
decoration, portions mirrored.
Leaded.

PS

Giberson
United States

65
Two Kinds of Animals
Finding Their Equilibrium
in Nature
H. 20.1 cm, D. 19.4 cm
Date: March 1978
Signature: Giberson/78
Amber tinted glass with trailed
and millefiori decoration, blown.
Fumed iridescent surface.

RL, WS, PS

66
Bowl with Green and
Pink Stripe
H. 18.2 cm, D. 16 cm
Date: February 1977
Colorless glass with trailed green
glass decoration, blown.

FS-G

67
Deco Vase
H. 9.6 cm, D. 8.3 cm
Date: 1978
Signature: ©JOHN GILMOR
GLASSWORKS 1978 1/25
Edition: 1/25
Aqua-tinted glass, blown. Sand-
blasted.

WS

68
Nouveau Vase
H. 11.1 cm, Depth 11.8 cm
Date: 1978
Signature: ©JOHN GILMOR
GLASSWORKS 1978 1/25
Aqua-tinted glass, blown. Sand-
blasted.

WS

69
Elefant
H. 22.1 cm, W. 18.9 cm,
Depth 7.6 cm
Date: 1977
Signature: Schä 77/Trademark;
GRAL/Mundgeblasem/Germany
(on paper label)
Designer: Helmut Schäffenacker
Maker: Livio Seguso
Edition: Limited to 200
Gray tinted glass, tooled.

FS-G, WS

Grossman
United States

70
Pooh-Dog's #1
H. 14.9 cm, D. 14.8 cm
Signature: J R Grossman/'77
Black amethyst glass, blown.
Sandblasted, copperplated.

WS, PS

71
Color Field
H. 66 cm, W. 66 cm
Date: March 18, 1978
Signature: Henry Halem 78
Gray tinted glass, sandblasted.
Amber glass leaded inset with
colored glass decoration.

RL, PS

Handler
United States

72
Wedding Breakfast
H. 36.8 cm, W. 40.6 cm,
Depth 31.4 cm
Date: March 1978
Signature: Audrey Handler 1978
Colored glass, blown; sterling
silver flatware and figures;
wooden table fabricated by Ron
Dekok, designed by Audrey
Handler.

PS

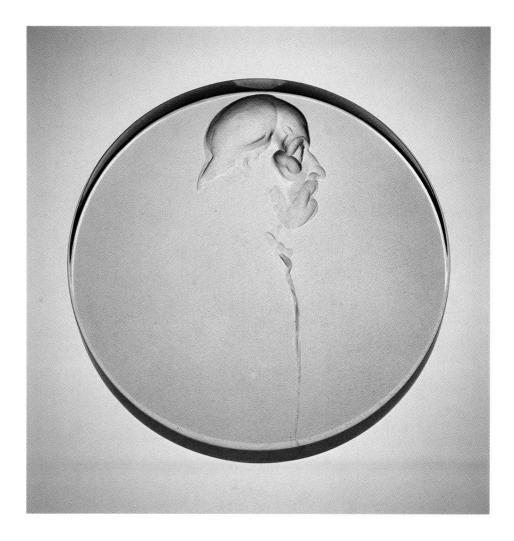

73
Bedřich Smetana
D. 15 cm, Depth 1.9 cm.
Date: February 1978
Signature: „B. Smetana" J Harcuba
1978
Colorless glass. Engraved.

PS

Harmon
United States

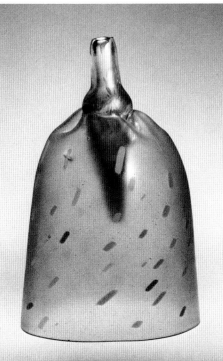

74
DV 1502
H. 21.4 cm, D. 15.4 cm
Date: October 1977
Signature: DV 1502 James P.
Harmon # 1777
Colorless glass with colored
decoration, blown. Two fused
forms. Fumed.

FS-G, WS, PS

94

75
2010 CSDV
H. 26.8 cm, D. 17.6 cm
Date: December 1977
Signature: 2010 CSDV James R.
Harmon–1977
Colorless glass with colored
decoration, blown. Two fused
forms. Fumed.

RL, PS

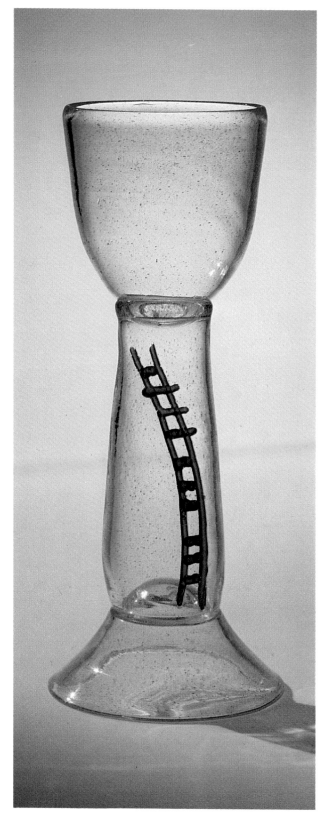

76
Included Ladder
H. 25 cm, D. 10.6 cm
Date: 1977
Signature: RICHARD HARNED
1977
Light green glass, blown.
Hollow stem contains
lampworked ladder.

FS-G, RL

77
Landscape
H. (approx.) 20.5 cm, D. 18.5 cm
Date: March 1978
Colorless glass encasing colored
glass decoration, blown.

FS-G

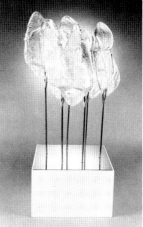

78
Eagle's Eye
H. (max.) 36 cm, W. 40 cm
Date: 1977
Signature: Lars Hellsten
Colorless glass, cast. Glass sphere
gathered and blocked. Mirror
base.

FS-G, RL, WS, PS

79
Frost Leaves
H. 142.2 cm, W. 68.6 cm
Date: 1977
Company: AB Orrefors Glasbruk
Colorless glass, cast. Three leaf
forms. Mirrored base.

RL, PS

Hilton
United Kingdom
Scotland (working in U.S.A.)

80
Spirit of the Hill
H. 47.5 cm, W. 70.8 cm,
Depth 70.9 cm
Date: 1977
Construction of wood, glass
sheets, and mirrors. Some parts
sandblasted. Concealed lighting.

PS

81
Crystal Glass Sculpture
H. (without base) 45 cm, L. 53 cm
Date: January 1978
Signature: P Hlava/Czech-
oslovakia
Colorless glass, blown. Cut and
assembled.

FS-G, RL, WS, PS

Hoeller
Federal Republic of Germany

82
Untitled
H. 14 cm, D. 13.8 cm
Date: April 1978
Colorless glass, blown. Cut and
polished.

FS-G

83
Landscape Study
H. 28 cm, D. 17.2 cm
Date: 1978
Signature: David R. Huchthausen
1978 BADEN bei WIEN No. 107
Colorless glass and colored glass
decoration in multiple layers,
blown.

PS

Hunkeler
Switzerland

84
Heaven, Sky, Earth and
Human-being
H. 9.1 cm, D. 6.2 cm
Date: August 1977
Signature: Reinhold Hunkeler/
8/1977/Hümiwel
Colorless glass with colored
decoration. Lampwork.

FS-G, RL

85
HØJBRO PLADS 5
H. 33.4 cm, W. 13 cm,
D. 8.7 cm
Date: February 1978
Signature: Monogram 78
Light aqua tinted glass, mold-
blown. Engraved.

FS-G, RL, WS, PS

Hurlstone
United States

86
Yin-Yang
H. 6.5 cm, D. 16.6 cm
Date: November 1977
Signature: R. W. Hurlstone
Edition: 1/1
Multi-colored glass, blown.
Fumed iridescent surface.

RL, PS

104

87
Blue Animal Bowl
H. 22.5 cm, D. 29.1 cm
Date: 1978
Signature: Boda/Unik 841/Ulrica
Edition: UNIK 841
Company: Kosta Boda AB
Colorless glass shaded to opalescent blue, blown. Enameled.

FS-G, RL, WS, PS

88 | 89
90 |

88
My Love
H. 26.3 cm, W. 13 cm, Depth
6.6 cm
Date: 1978
Signature: Boda/Unik 842/Ulrica
Edition: Unik 842
Company: Kosta Boda AB
Colorless glass, mold-blown.
Enameled.

RL, PS

90
Flying Dragons Pokal
H. 29.3 cm, D. 11.6 cm
Date: 1978
Signature: Boda/Unik 845/Ulrica.
Handmade/Boda/Sweden (on
paper label)
Edition: Unik 845
Company: Kosta Boda AB
Colorless glass, blown. Enameled.

RL

89
Running Red Horses in
Green Field
H. 30.6 cm, W. 19.4 cm,
Depth. 9.4 cm
Date: 1978
Signature: Boda/Unik 844/Ulrica
Edition: Unik 844
Company: Kosta Boda AB
Colorless glass, mold-blown. Ena-
meled decoration.

FS-G, WS, PS

91 a-j
**Tiberius 826 (tumbler
set of ten objects)**
H. (tallest) 22.6 cm, D. 10 cm
Date: 1976
Signature: Ichendorf/handarbeit
(on paper label)
Pale blue tinted glass, blown.

RL, WS, PS

Ipsen
United States

92
Baptismal Font
H. 7 cm, D. 64.5 cm
Date: May 1978
Signature: Ipsen 1978
Colorless glass with orange
decoration, cast.

RL, PS

93
Vision II
H. 50.8 cm, W. 38.5 cm
Date: 1978
Opaque white and colorless
glass with etched blue decoration.
Leaded.

PS

Jelínek
Czechoslovakia

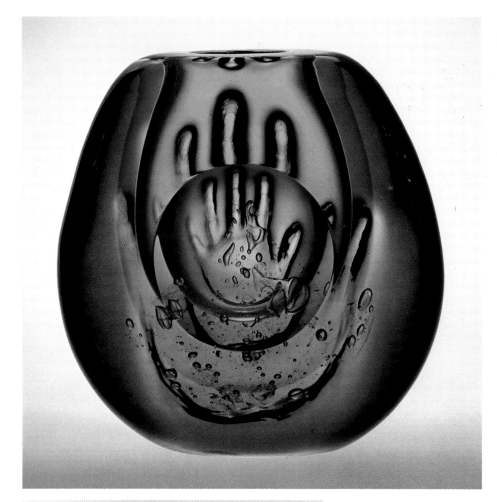

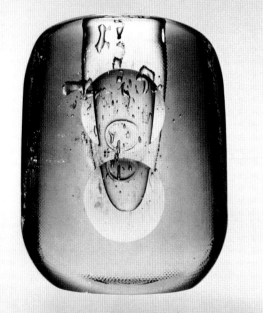

94
Mother and Child
H. 21.5 cm, W. 22.2 cm, Depth
12.1 cm
Date: February 1978
Signature: V. Jelínek
Green tinted glass encased with
amber tinted glass, blown;
molded impression. Cut.

WS

95
Crystal Object
H. 23 cm, W. 18.3 cm, Depth 10.6
cm
Date: January 1978
Signature: V. Jelínek
Colorless glass, blown; textured
surface with impressed decora-
tion. Cut.

FS-G, RL, WS, PS

96, 97 a-l
Set of Drinking Glasses
(two forms)
H. 12.5 cm, D. 8.1 cm
Date: February 1977
Colorless glass, mold-blown.

WS, PS

Johansson
Sweden

98
Plate Orrefors J 956-78
H. 9.9 cm, D. 35.1 cm
Date: January 1978
Signature: Orrefors Expo J 956/78
Jan Johansson
Company: AB Orrefors Glasbruk
Colorless glass, blown. Cut and
acid-etched.

RL, PS

99
Spiral Disc
H. 38.1 cm, D. 36.2 cm
Date: 1976
Signature: Hadeland, W.J.
Company: Hadelands Glassverk
Deep blue and amethyst glass,
cased with colorless glass, blown.

FS-G, RL

Kagami Crystal Glass Works Ltd.
Japan

100 a-e
Tableware
W. (largest) 40.3 cm
Date: April 1976
Signature: Kagami/Trademark/
G/Crystal/Made/in/Japan
Designer: Wataru Hayashi
Colorless glass, pressed.

RL, PS

101
Nine Panels
H. 102.2 cm, W. 80.3 cm,
Depth 46.5 cm
Date: May 1976
Signature: Benjamin/Kaiser/1978
Nine separate aquamarine-tinted
laminated blocks. Ground and
sandblasted. Mirrored pedestal
base with concealed light.

RL, WS, PS

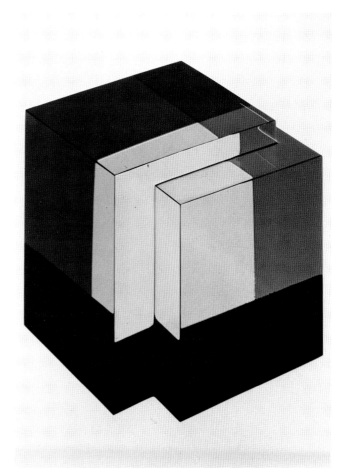

◄102
Penetration
H. 20.2 cm, Depth 29.9 cm
Date: March 1978
Signature: MARIAN KAREL 78
Colorless glass. Cut and polished.
Two parts.

FS-G, PS

103
Bauhaus 77
H. 16.9 cm, W. 17.1 cm
Date: March 1977
Signature: MARIAN KAREL
Aquamarine tinted glass. Cut and
polished.

WS

104
Stretching
H. 19.5 cm, W. 17.4 cm, L. 25.4 cm
Date: July 1976
Signature: 76 MARIAN KAREL
Colorless glass. Cut and polished.

FS-G

Kaspar
Federal Republic of Germany

105
Wotan's-Oak-Tree
H. 44.9 cm, W. 46.7 cm
Date: December 1977
Signature: 77 Peter Kaspar
Colorless glass, poured and
shaped.

FS-G, RL, WS

106
Frost Queen
H. 29.2 cm, D. 20.4
Date: March 1978
Signature: E. Katona '78
White glass cased with shades of
deep blue tinted glass, blown.

FS-G

Kawakami
Japan

107
Crystal Bowl
H. 8.9 cm, W. 22 cm,
Depth 21.6 cm
Date: June 1976
Company: Hoya Corporation
Yellow tinted glass, mold-spun.
Cut and polished.

PS

108
Composition XXIX
H. (with frame) 79.4 cm, W. 81.7
cm
Date: February 1976
Signature: XXIX/RK 2/76
Opaque white and colored flat
glass with appliqués. Sheet of
colorless glass projects from
surface. Leaded.

RL, WS, PS

109
**Wake Me When We
Get There**
H. 120 cm, W. 81 cm
Date: 1976
Colored and colorless glass.
Sandblasted. Leaded.

WS, PS

*Artist's slide. Object broken in
transit; not shown in exhibition.*

110
Young American
H. 14.5 cm, D. 13.5 cm
Date: October 1977
Signature: Russell Kelly/'78
Edition: 1/1
Opaque white glass with colored decoration, cased with colorless glass, blown.

FS-G, RL, WS

111▶
Untitled
H. 25.5 cm, D. 14.3 cm
Date: July 1977
Signature: R. Kelly '77
Edition: 1/1
Opaque white glass with trailed orange tinted glass decoration, overlaid with colorless glass, blown.

FS-G, WS

Kerrn-Jespersen
Denmark

112 a-d
Four Tall Snapglasses
with Color in Stem
H. 21.8 cm, D. 4.5 cm
Date: January 1977
Signature: Monogram
Colorless glass with colored glass
decoration, blown.

FS-G

113 a-d
Crystal Wineglasses
with Purple
H. 12.3 cm, D. 7.8 cm
Date: March 1978
Signature: Monogram
Colorless glass with colored glass
inclusions, blown.

FS-G

114
Bowl with White Thread Decorations.
H. 14 cm
Date: 1977
Colorless glass with white thread decoration. Lampwork.

RL, WS, PS

Artist's slide. Object delayed in transit at date of publication.

Krebs
Federal Republic of Germany

115 a-c
Gedankensplitter
H. 27 cm, D. 7.9 cm
Date: 1977
Signature: Ernst Krebs /77/
München abc (signature on c)
Edition: 1/1
Colorless glass, mold-blown.
Engraved.

WS

116a-c
His and Hers
H. (tallest) 25.1 cm, W. 13.4 cm
Date: February 19, 1978
Signature: David Kroeger/'78
Light amber tinted glass, blown.

WS

117
Little Rock River
H. (largest rock) 15.8 cm; overall
size about 75 cm x 75 cm
Date: January 1978
Signature: JON/KUHN/JAN 1978
Colored glass, rolled while hot in
chemicals to coat the surface. One
cut to reveal interior. Sand.

FS-G, WS, PS

118 a-c
Sport Prizes for
Weight Lifters
H. (of a) 43.1 cm, W. 13.6 cm
Date: 1977
Colorless glass, mold-blown. Cut.

RL, WS, PS

Labino
United States

119
Triangular Fountain
H. 18.9 cm. W. 11.2 cm
Date: March 1978
Signature: Labino/1978
Colorless glass, multiple overlay
technique. Colored inclusions.

WS

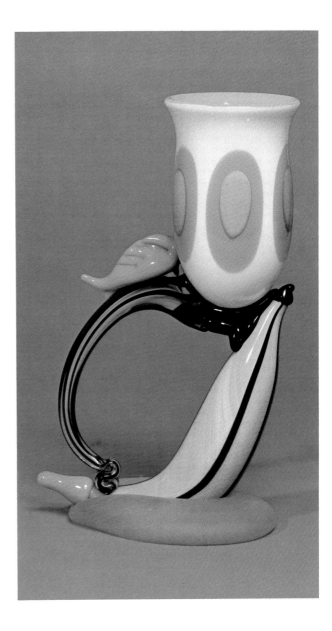

120
A Cup with Appeal # 2
H. 21.7 cm, W. 13.4
Date: 1977
Signature: Robert Levin 1977
Colored glass, blown. Trailed and
applied decoration.

PS

Libenský & Brychtová
Czechoslovakia

121 a-c
Cylinder in Spheric Space.
D. 30.1 cm
Date: 1977
Signature: LIB-BRY-77
Nearly colorless glass, cast. Cut.
Three parts.

PS

122
Erosionware
H. 22 cm, D. 14.5 cm
Date: January 1978
Colorless glass, blown.
Sandblasted.

RL, WS

Lipofsky
United States

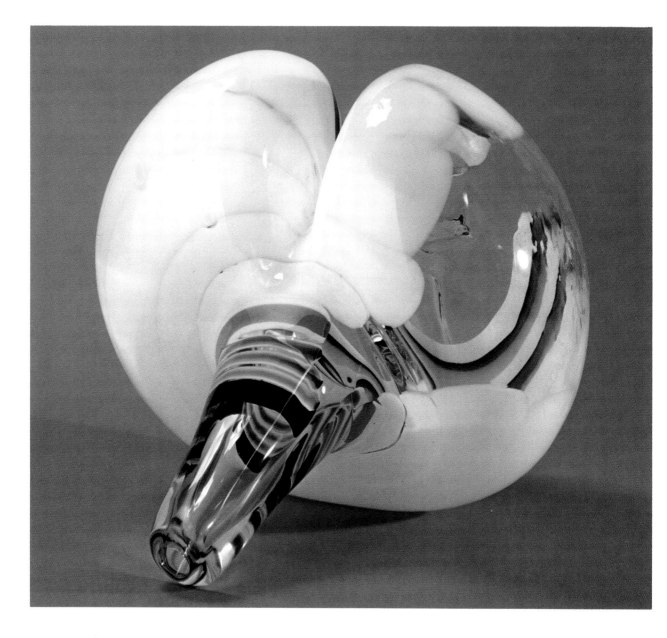

123
Serie Fratelli Toso 1977
H. 31.4 cm, W. 38.5 cm,
Depth 40.7 cm
Date: Completed 1978
Signature: Lipofsky/'78
Made with the help of Gianni
Toso.
Opaque white glass with colored
glass decoration. Cased with
colorless glass, partly mold-
blown.

WS, PS

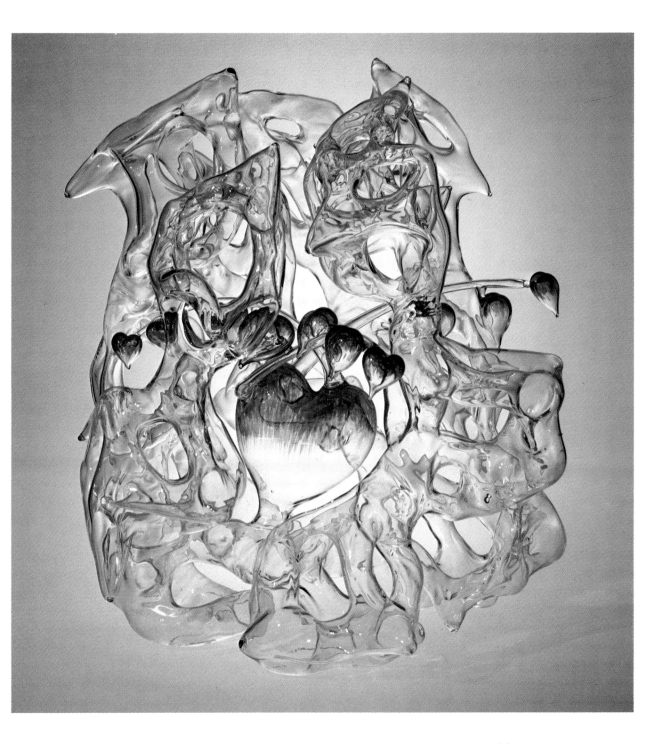

124
Birth of a Star
H. 53 cm, W. 43 cm
Date: November 1977
Signature: Věra Lišková/1978
Colorless and ruby-tinted glass.
Lampwork.

RL, WS, PS

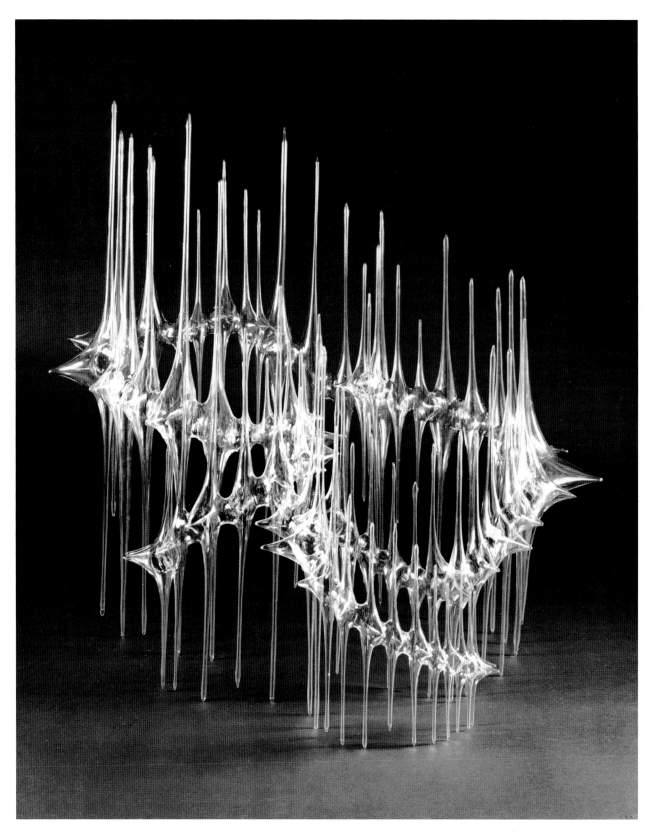

◄125
Anthem of Joy in Glass
H. 99.5 cm, W. 91.5 cm
Date: September 1977
Signature: Věra Lišková/1977
Colorless glass. Lampwork.

RL, WS, PS

Not traveling in exhibition.

126
Inverted Tube/Cut Line
H. 33.4 cm, W. 41.3 cm
Date: 1977
Signature: Harvey K. Littleton
1977/©
Colorless glass, cased with white
and red tinted glass, blown. Cut
and polished.

PS

J & L Lobmeyr
Austria

127 a-d
Wine Set
H. (goblet) 15.3 cm, D. 5.5 cm
Date: Made 1978; designed
December 1977
Signature: Monogram
Designer: Peter Rath
Colorless glass, mold-blown.

RL

128
Bluebells
H. 13.6 cm, D. 13.6 cm
Date: January 1978
Signature: F. L. 78/N. G. 8
Colorless glass enclosing colored
glass decoration, blown.

FS-G

Lynggaard
Denmark

129
Rainbow Stripes II
H. 14.2 cm, D. 14.3 cm
Date: February 1978
Signature: F. L. 78/N. G.10
Colorless glass with internal
colored glass decoration, blown.
Fumed iridescent surfaces.

RL, PS

130
Paeonia Bowl
H. 19.1 cm, D. 20.4 cm
Date: November 1977
Signature: F. L. 77/N. G. 5
Colorless glass with colored glass
decoration, blown.

FS-G

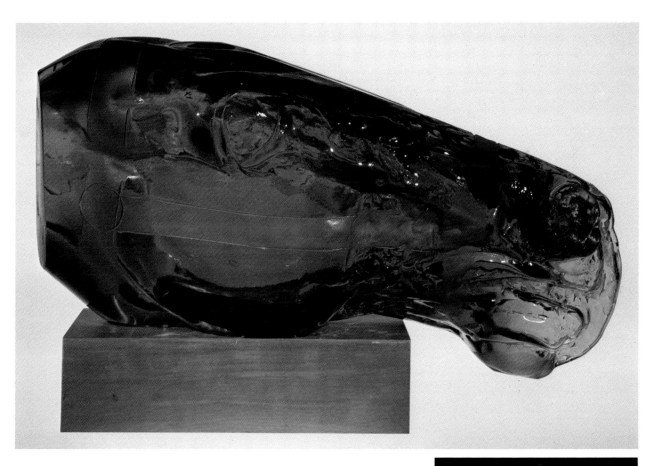

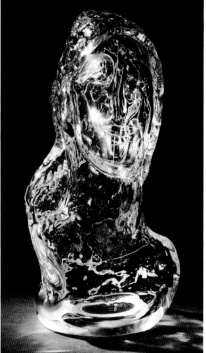

131
Head of a Horse
H. (with base) 23.3 cm, L. 38.9 cm
Date: December 1977
Signature: MACHAC 77
Amber tinted glass, blown into
plaster mold. Cut, engraved.

WS

132
Head of a Woman
H. 41.3 cm, W. 22.6 cm
Date: November 1977
Signature: MACHAC 77
Colorless glass, blown into plaster
mold. Cut, engraved.

PS

Maderna
Austria

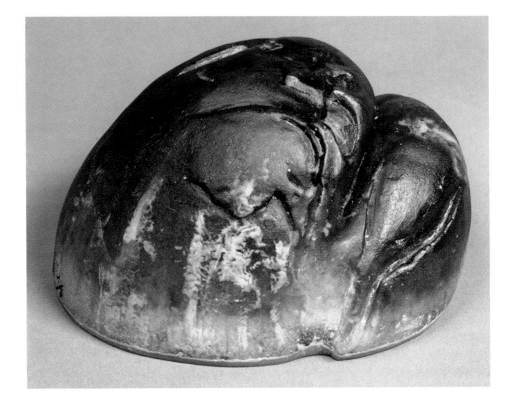

133
Bald
H. 9.4 cm, W. 16.4 cm
Date: 1977
Signature: MARIANNE
MADERNA/1/7
Edition: 1/7
Pâte-de-verre.

FS-G, RL

142

**134a-c
Blackbird Scent Bottles**
H. (tallest) 6.5 cm, D. 4 cm
Date: May 1977
Colorless glass bottles with
colored glass decoration on stop-
pers. Lampwork.

FS-G, WS

143

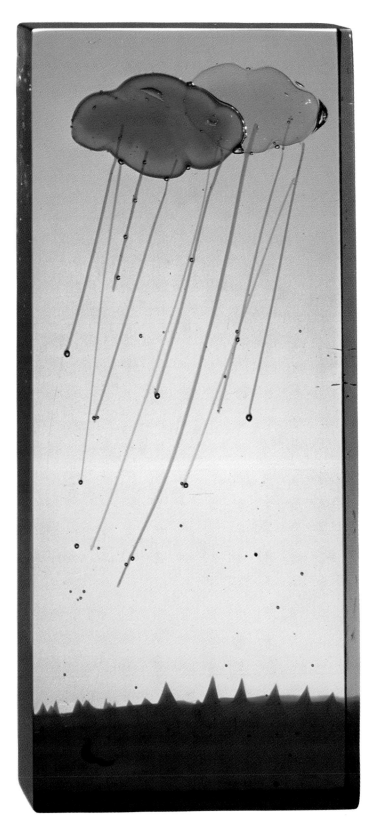

135
**Nature and Geometry—
Clouds**
H. 40.8 cm, W. 18 cm,
Depth 5.2 cm
Signature: Federica Marangoni '77
Colorless glass enclosing blue
glass decoration, cast. Cut.

FS-G, WS

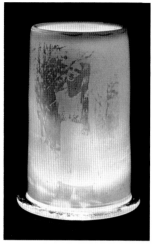

136
High School Sweetheart
H. 20.3 cm, D. 14.4 cm
Date: 1978
Signature: High School/Sweet-
heart/©/Marioni/ '78
Edition: 1/1
Assisted by Gary Beecham and
John Littleton.
Opaque white glass with pho-
tographic emulsion, cased with
colorless glass, blown.

PS

137
200 years
H. 79.5 cm, W. 48.7 cm
Date: 1976
Signature: 200 years© Edition: 1/1
Made with the assistance of Hans
and Werner Gewohn.
Opalescent glass with colored
decoration.
This piece was made possible by a
grant from the N.E.A.

RL

Marodić
Yugoslavia

138
Suddenly, I Was Con-
fronted with the Truth...
H. 19.4 cm, D. 31 cm
Date: 1978
Colorless glass, blown.

FS-G, WS, PS

139
Non-Functional
Checkerboard Teapot
H. 12.3 cm, W. 14.5 cm
Date: May 1977
Signature: © 1978/Marquis
Assisted by Jody Fine and Janis
Miltenberger.
Colored glass mosaic, fused and
blown.

RL, PS

Martens
Belgium

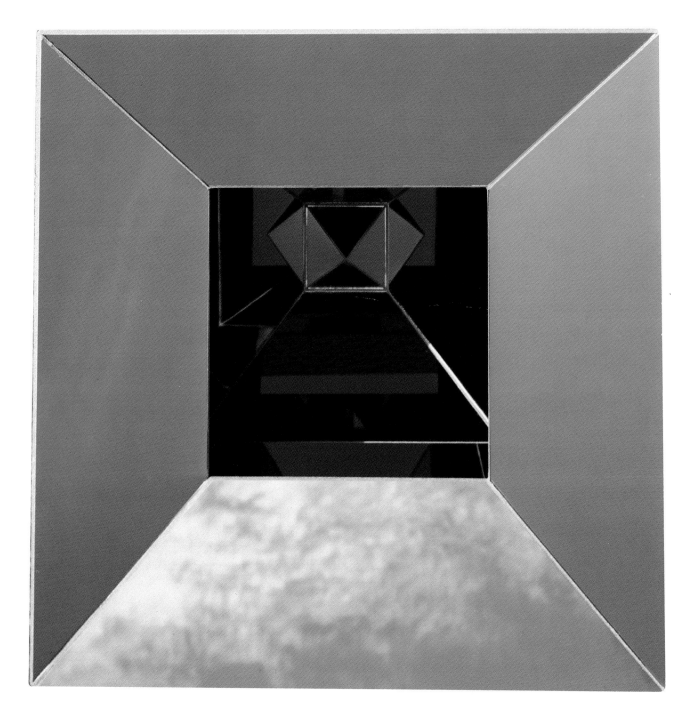

140
Boite-Plomp, Bleu et Vert
H. 39.3 cm, W. 60.7 cm, Depth
60.7 cm
Signature: MICHEL MARTENS/7712
Foam and steel form, covered
with glass mirrors.

PS

141
Untitled
H. 18.5 cm, W. 31.1 cm
Date: 1976
Signature: MARTINUZZI/PAOLO
Colorless glass, blown. Scratch
engraved. Wooden base.

FS-G, PS

Martinuzzi
Italy

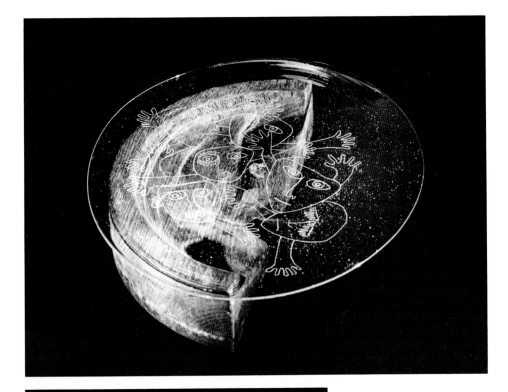

142
Untitled
H. (with base) 6.1 cm, D. 29 cm
Date: 1977
Signature: MARTINUZZI/PAOLO
Colorless glass, blown. Scratch
engraved. Wooden base.

FS-G, RL, WS

143
Untitled
H. 21.3 cm, W. 21.7 cm
Date: 1977
Signature: Martinuzzi Paolo
Colorless glass, blown. Scratch
engraved. Wooden base.

RL, WS, PS

144
Color Field Vase
H. 21.3 cm, D. 12.2 cm
Date: 1978
Signature: Tom McGlauchlin/1978
Colorless glass with colored
decoration, blown.

RL

151

Meitner
United States

145 a-c
Three Small Cylinders
with Stoppers
H. (tallest) 11.3 cm, D. 2.8 cm
Date: March 1978
Signature: R. Meitner 78
(signature on a)
Colorless glass, cased with
opaque white glass layer. Colored
thread decoration, blown.

WS, PS

146 ▶
Nike '78
H. 51.9 cm, W. 39 cm
Date: 1978
Plate glass, sagged.

RL, WS, PS

Meydam
Netherlands

147
Unique Piece 77180
H. 31.6 cm, D. 16.2 cm
Date: 1977
Signature: LEERDAM UNICA MAE
180"F Meydam
Company: Leerdam
Colorless, amber tinted and
opalescent red glass, blown.

PS

148 | 149
‾ | 150

148
Unique Piece 78103
H. 18.1 cm, W. 18.2 cm,
Depth 18.2 cm
Date: February 1978
Signature: LEERDAM UNICA
FM78103/F Meydam
Company: Leerdam
Light green and gray tinted plate
glass. Cut and cemented.

PS

149
Unique Piece 75186
H. 13.8 cm, D. 27 cm
Date: 1976
Signature: LEERDAM UNICA MAE
186″F Meydam
Company: Leerdam
Colorless glass, blown. Red opal
glass inside.

PS

150
Unique Piece 78089
H. 19.6 cm, D. 26.4 cm
Date: February 1978
Signature: LEERDAM UNICA
FM78089″F Meydam
Company: Leerdam
Colorless and opaque white and
gray glass, blown.

RL

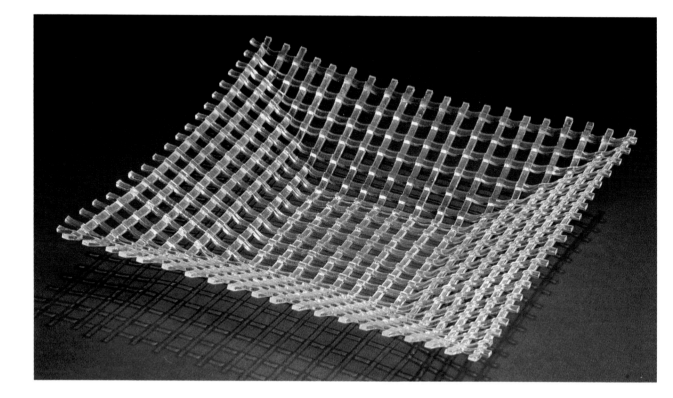

151
Open Squares
H. 5.1 cm, W. 39 cm,
Depth 39.1 cm
Date: February 1978
Signature: STEVE MILDWOFF 78
Colorless glass strips, bent and
fused in a stainless steel mold.

FS-G, RL

152
Mosaik Glass Bowl
H. 5.7 cm, W. 30.7 cm
Date: November 1977
Signature: MOJE/1977
Colored glass canes, fused. Cut.

WS, PS

Moje
Federal Republic of Germany

153
Mosaik Glass Bowl
H. 5.9 cm, D. 18.3 cm,
Date: February 1978
Signature: MOJE/1977
Colored glass canes, fused. Cut.

FS-G, RL

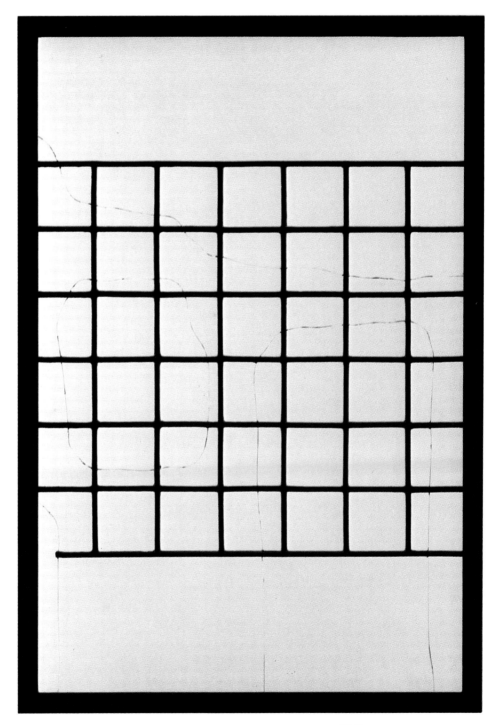

154
Untitled
H. (with frame) 82.1 cm,
W. 56.7 cm
Date: 1977
Signature: PETER MOLLICA 1977
Colorless glass. Leaded.

FS-G, RL, WS, PS

Mollica
United States

155
Untitled
H. (with frame) 82.4 cm,
W. 57.1 cm
Date: 1977
Signature: PETER MOLLICA 1977
Opalescent and green glass.
Sandblasted. Leaded.

FS-G, WS

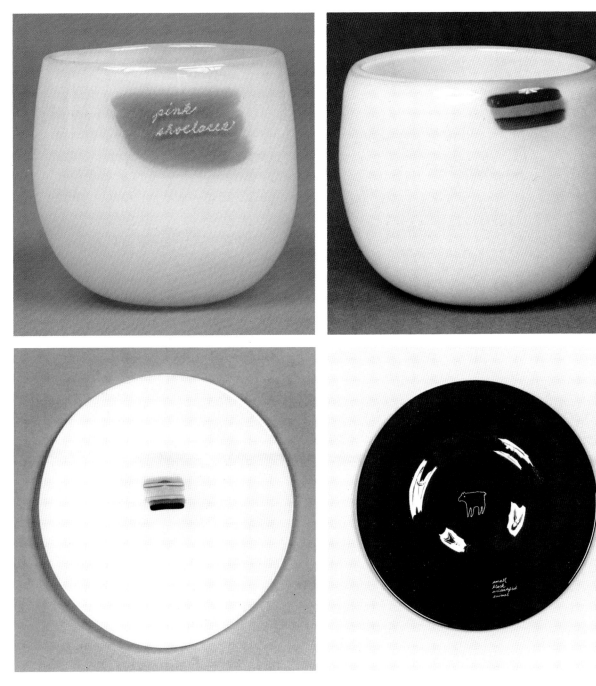

156
Pink Shoelaces Cup
H. 7 cm, D. 7.8 cm
Date: 1977
Signature: n. monk
Blown by Paul Koller.
Opalescent glass with colored decoration, cased with colorless glass, blown. Scratch engraved inscription.

PS

157
Seersucker Cup
H. 6.6 cm, D. 8 cm
Date: 1977
Signature: n. monk
Blown by Paul Koller
Opaque white glass with colored decoration, cased with colorless glass, blown.

FS-G, WS

158
Stripe Plate
H. 1.6 cm, D. 25 cm
Date: 1977
Signature: n. monk 77
Blown by Paul Koller.
Opalescent glass with colored decoration, cased with colorless glass, blown.

FS-G, RL, WS

159
Small Black Unidentified Animal Plate
H. 1.1 cm, D. 21.4 cm
Date: 1977
Signature: n. monk 77
Blown by Paul Koller
Black amber glass, blown.
Engraved.

WS, PS

156 | 157
158 | 159

Moore
United States

160
Amber Platter
H. 8.9 cm, D. 52.8 cm
Signature: Benjamin P. Moore
Colorless glass, shaded, blown.
Fumed rim.

PS

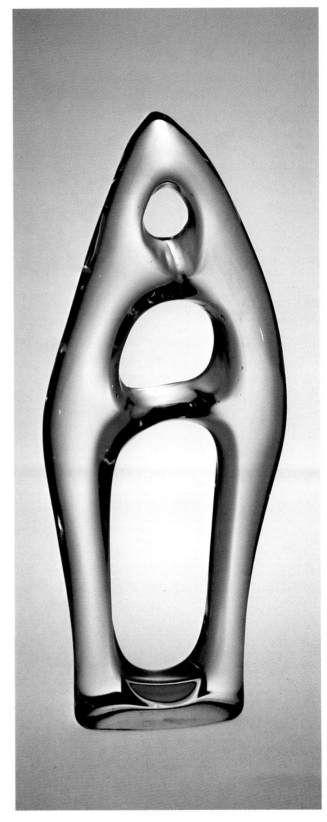

161
**Figure of Woman on
Negative Space**
H. 53.5 cm, W. 22.9 cm
Date: 1977
Signature: Roberto Moretti
Light blue tinted glass cased with
colorless glass.

WS

162
Shamrock Chalice
H. 33.2 cm, D. 6.5 cm
Date: January 1978
Signature: Scott Mundt '1978'
Colorless and light green tinted
glass, blown.

FS-G

163
Whirlybird
H. 34.3 cm, D. 6.1 cm
Date: January 1978
Signature: Scott Mundt/'1978'/
Colorless and deep red tinted
glass, blown.

FS-G, RL, WS, PS

164
Two of Clubs
H. 28.4 cm, D. 6.5 cm
Date: January 1978
Signature: Scott Mundt '1978'
Colorless and ruby tinted glass,
blown.

RL, WS, PS

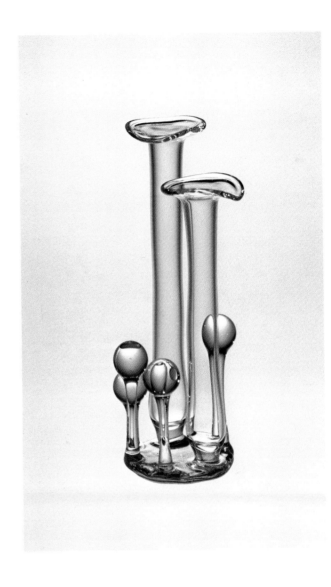

165
Grass Holder with Fungi
H. 10.8 cm, W. 5.7 cm
Date: November 1977
Colorless glass. Lampwork.

FS-G, WS

Musler
United States

166
Woven Bowl
H. 11.8 cm, D. 18.7 cm
Date: December 1977
Signature: Jay Musler
Colorless glass, blown. Engraved,
sandblasted, rubbed with earth-
colored pigments for contrast.

RL

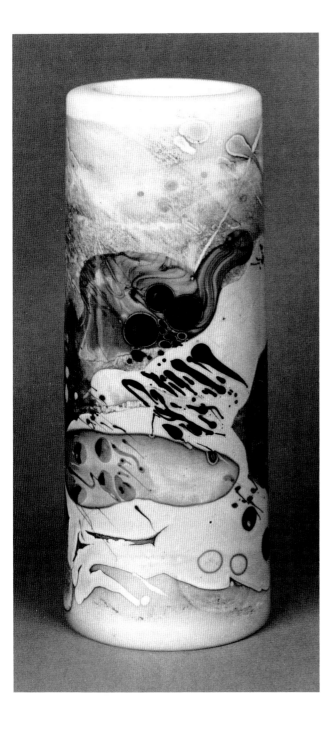

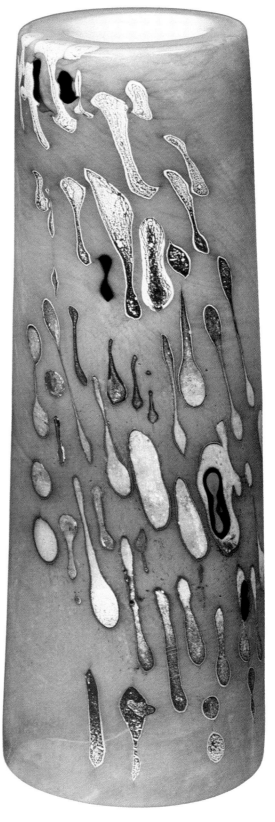

167
Blue Field on White
H. 25.7 cm, D. 10.4 cm
Date: 1976
Signature: Joel Philip Myers 1976
White opalescent glass with
colored glass decoration, blown.

RL

168
White on White Field
H. 25 cm, D. 9.3 cm
Date: 1976
Signature: Joel Philip Myers 1976
White opalescent glass with
colored glass decoration, blown.

PS

Neuman
United States

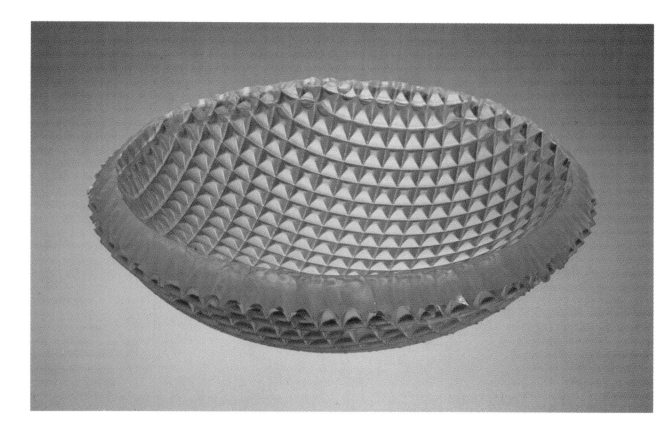

169
Grid Bowl
H. 7.8 cm, D. 29.5 cm
Date: March 1977
Pale green tinted glass, slump
cast. Sandblasted.

FS-G

170
Engraved Bottle
H. 45.4 cm, D. 7.5 cm
Date: March 1978
Signature: Nickerson 1978
Pale aqua tinted glass, blown.
Ground and engraved.

RL, WS

Nieswaag
United States

171
Untitled
H. 8.4 cm, W. 20.6 cm,
Depth 11.5 cm
Date: February 7, 1978
Signature: Jim Nieswaag/1978
Colorless glass with colored
decoration, blown into wooden
mold.

FS-G, RL, WS

172
Flower
H. 27.9 cm, W. 28.4 cm
Date: November 1977
Signature: B. NOVÁ JUNIOR
Amber tinted glass. Cut and
polished.

RL, PS

Oliva
Czechoslovakia

173
Colored Vase
H. 26.9 cm, D. 9.5 cm
Date: July 1976
Signature: Oliva
Colorless glass with colored glass
decoration, blown.

RL

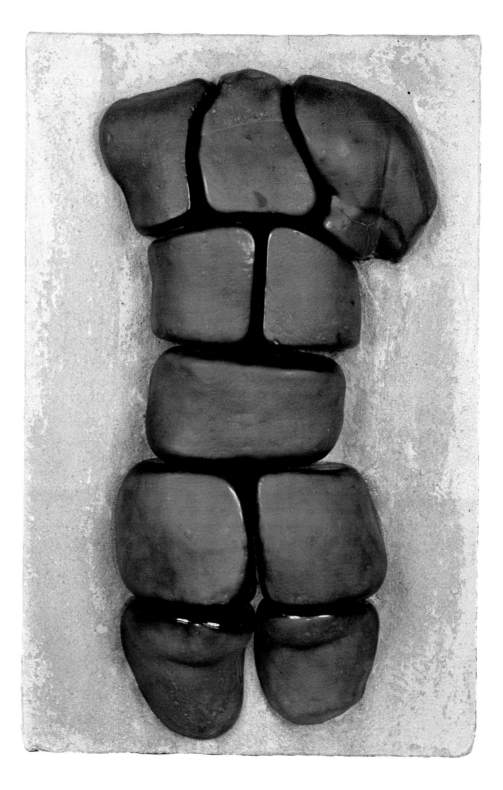

174
Torso II
H. (of block) 101.5 cm, W. 66 cm
Date: 1976
Edition: 2/2
Black glass, mold-blown. Etched.
Set in a concrete block.

RL, WS

175
Banded Bronze
H. 17.2 cm, W. 17.8 cm,
Depth 17.7 cm
Date: 1976
Signature: Patti '76
Colored and colorless sheet glass,
laminated and blown.

PS

176
Wisteria Trees, PWV 079
H. 29.4 cm, D. 27 cm
Date: 1978
Signature: MARK PEISER PWV
079-1978
Colorless glass encasing lamp-
work decoration, blown.

FS-G, RL, PS

Pennell
United Kingdom
England

177
Major Egmont Brodie-
Williams and the
Crocodiles
H. 15.6 cm, D. 7.7 cm
Date: 1977
Signature: Monogram
Edition: 1/25
Colorless glass, blown. Engraved.

FS-G, RL, WS, PS

178
Cascando I
H. 25.1 cm, W. 43.1 cm
Date: January 1977
Signature: R E Pietruszewski '77
Gray or black glass. Stacked,
fused.

FS-G

Pietruszewski
United States

179
Totem
H. 68.5 cm, D. 10.1 cm
Date: December 1976
Signature: R E Pietruszewski-'76
Colorless glass. Lampwork.

RL, WS, PS

180
Conjunction II
H. 43 cm, D. 10.9 cm
Date: March 1978
Signature: R E Pietruszewski
© 1978
Colorless glass. Lampwork.

FS-G, RL, WS

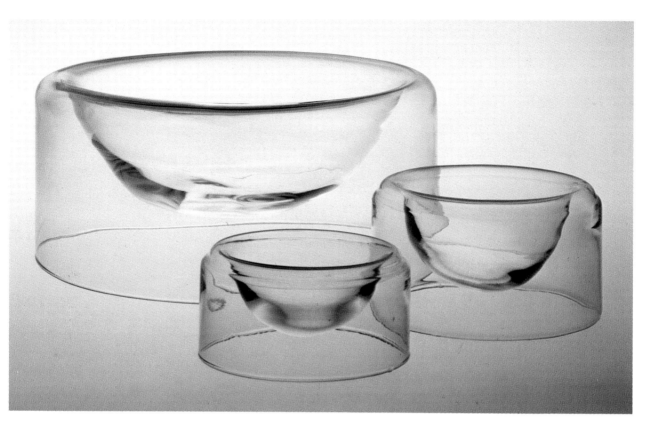

181 a-c
Galaxy Salad Set
H. (tallest) 12.7 cm, D. 29.3 cm
Date: Made February 1978
Signature: KITCHEN/CHEMIS-
TRY/trademark/HAND-
BLOWN/PILGRIM/GLASS (on
paper label)
Designers: Edward P. Kaeding
and Edward F. Whiting
Colorless glass, blown.

PS

Pliva
Czechoslovakia

182 a-c
Cylinder
H. 28.2 cm, W. 21.4 cm
Date: December 1977
Signature: PLIVA 77
Colorless glass, optical quality.
Cut and polished. Three parts.

RL, WS, PS

183a-i
Column
H. 59.7 cm, D. 19.7 cm
Date: September 1977
Signature: PLIVA 77
Colorless glass, optical quality.
Cut and polished. Nine parts.

FS-G, WS, PS

184a-b
Pyramid
H. 25 cm, W. 28 cm
Date: January 1978
Signature: P78
Colorless glass. Cut and polished.
Two parts.

RL

185
Ovoid
H. 11.2 cm, D. 18.6 cm
Date: April 1977
Signature: OLDRICH PLIVA 77
Colorless glass. Ground and
polished.

FS-G, RL

Popa
Romania

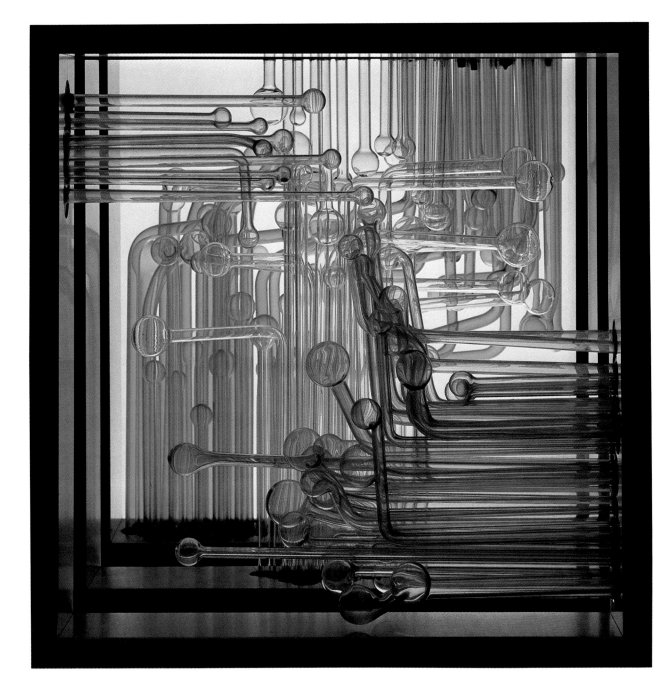

186 a-c
Treble Screen
H. 45 cm, W. 45 cm
Date: 1978
Colored glass lampwork; aluminum over wood frames. Three parts.

RL, PS

187
**Another Look at My Beef
with the Government**
H. 69 cm, W. 82 cm
Date: 1976
Colored glass; photographic
transparency. Sandblasted. Leaded.

RL

189 | 191

190

◄**188**
Nightmare #1
H. 123 cm x W. 91 cm
Date: 1977-1978
Colored and opalescent textured
flat glass with lenses and x-ray
photograph. Leaded.

PS

189
Rheingold *Pokal* 0,2
H. 18 cm, D. 7.1 cm
Date: February 14, 1977
Signature: MADE/IN/GERMANY
(on paper label)
Designer: Hermann Hoffmann
Colorless glass, blown.

WS

190
Maxim
H. 16.4 cm, D. 9.5 cm
Date: October 27, 1976
Signature: MADE/IN/GERMANY
(on paper label)
Designer: Hermann Hoffmann
Colorless glass, blown.

WS

191
Günz
H. 17.3 cm, D. 8.2 cm
Date: August 19, 1977
Signature: MADE/IN/GERMANY
(on paper label)
Designer: Hermann Hoffmann
Colorless glass, blown.

WS

Reusch
Canada

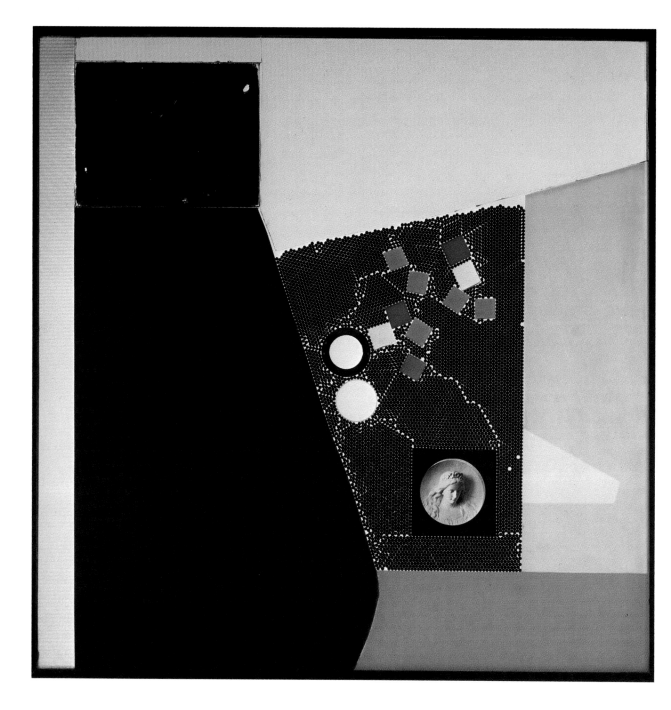

192
3000 Ball Bearings
H. 61.4 cm, W. 61.3 cm
Date: 1977
Two colorless sheets of glass
enclosing ball bearings, a glass
lantern slide, lenses and flat glass.
Some portions sandblasted.

RL, PS

186

193
Prince
H. 86.8 cm, W. 86.3 cm
Date: 1976
Flat glass, some textured, incorporating an optical lens, prism, and glass lantern slide. Some portions sandblasted. Leaded.

FS-G, WS, PS

Riedel
Austria

195 a-j
Sommeliers
H. (tallest) 24.5 cm
Date: 1976 to 1978
Signature: Monogram
Designer: Claus J. Riedel
Colorless glass, blown. Hand
formed stem.

FS-G, RL, WS

▲
194a-c
Adam and Eve
H. (tallest) 24.9 cm
Date: c. 1977
Signature: Monogram
Designer: Claus J. Riedel
Colorless glass. Hand pressed
stem, blown bowl.

WS

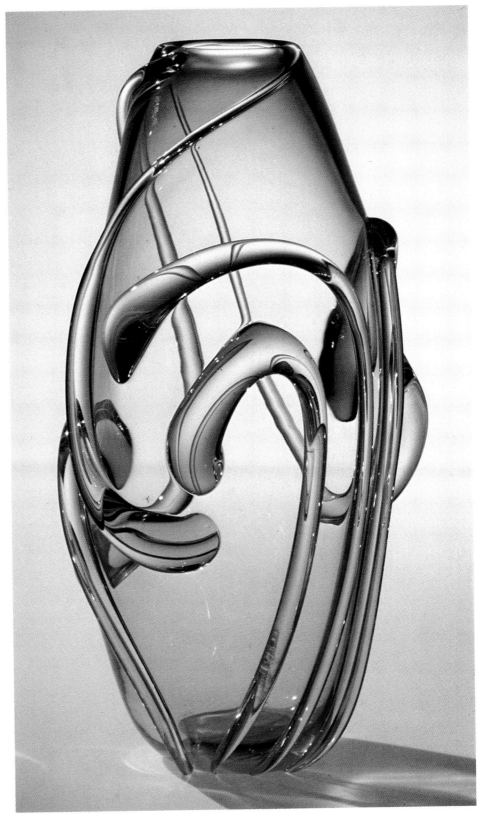

196
Free-form Appliqué Vase #3
H. 21.4 cm, D. 12.7 cm
Date: November 1977
Signature: RFAG-77
Colorless glass with applied
decoration, blown.

RL

Rosenthal Aktiengesellschaft
Federal Republic of Germany

197 a-i
Papyrus
H. (tallest) 24.2 cm, D. 5.4 cm
Date: 1976
Signature: Rosenthal/Studio-linie
Colorless glass bowl, blown. Light
yellow-green tinted glass stem
and base, hand applied.

FS-G, WS

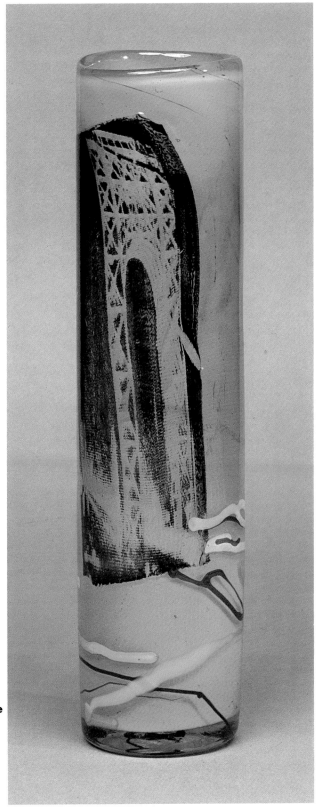

198
George Washington Bridge
H. 30.6 cm, D. 7.7 cm
Date: April 1977
Signature: Rothenfeld/77
Opalescent flat glass with photo/
silkscreen enameled onto surface
and marvered into blown form.
Applied colored glass decoration.

RL

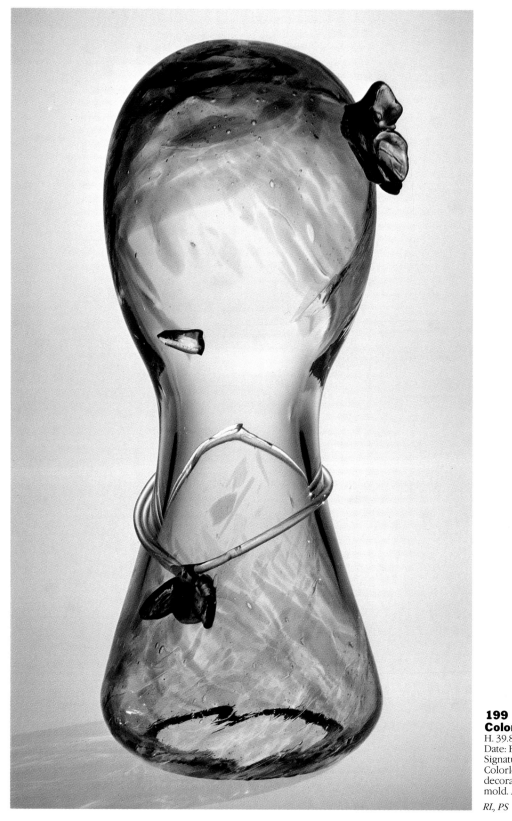

199
Colored Head with Flower
H. 39.8 cm, D. (base) 16.6 cm
Date: February 1977
Signature: M. Roubíčková 1977
Colorless glass with colored glass
decoration, blown into plaster
mold. Applied decoration.

RL, PS

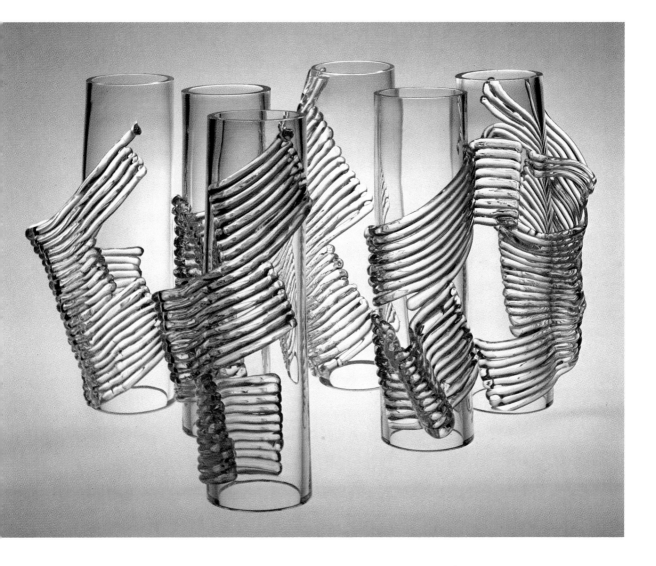

200 a-f
Stream
H. 34.6 cm, W. 15.6 cm
Date: March 1978
Signature: Rozsypal 1978
„STREAM"/oI (on a)
Colorless glass, blown. Applied
colorless glass decoration. Six
parts.

FS-G, RL, WS

Cristalería San Carlos S.A.
Argentina

201
Pote Machareti 345—
Guanacos Relief
H. 23.8 cm, D. 23 cm
Date: Made January 1977;
designed September 1976
Signature: CRISTAL/SAN CAR-
LOS/MADE IN ARGENTINA
(paper label)
Designers: Anselmo Gaminara
and Ricardo Weisl
Colorless glass, cased with ruby-
red tinted glass, blown. Sand-
blasted.

RL, WS, PS

202
Pote Chiriguano 349—
Owl Relief
H. 36.4 cm, D. 33.7 cm
Date: Made January 1978;
designed September 1976
Signature: CRISTAL/SAN CAR-
LOS/MADE IN ARGENTINA
(paper label)
Designers: Anselmo Gaminara
and Ricardo Weisl
Colorless glass, cased with cobalt
blue tinted glass, blown. Sand-
blasted.

WS

203 | 205
204 | 206

203
Spring
Four Seasons Series
H. 3.9 cm, D. 37.8 cm
Signature: venini italia Laura
100/15
Company: Venini & Co.
Colorless and green tinted glass,
blown. Ground.

FS-G, PS

204
Summer
Four Seasons Series
H. 3.6 cm, D. 38.2 cm
Signature: venini italia Laura
100/24
Company: Venini & Co.
Colorless, red, green and yellow
tinted glass, blown. Ground.

FS-G, PS

205
Fall
Four Seasons Series
H. 3.5 cm, D. 38 cm
Signature: venini italia Laura
100/27
Company: Venini & Co.
Colorless, amber and brown
tinted glass, blown. Ground.

FS-G, PS

206
Winter
Four Seasons Series
H. 4.4 cm, D. 37.9 cm
Signature: venini italia Laura
100/23
Company: Venini & Co.
Colorless, blue and white tinted
glass, blown. Ground.

FS-G, PS

207
Numeri
H. 3.5 cm, D. 27.3 cm
Signature: venini italia 1088/74
Company: Venini & Co.
Colorless and colored glass
mosaic canes, fused. Ground.

PS

208
Crystal Vase
H. 30.1 cm, W. 12.6 cm
Date: January 1976
Company: Hoya Corporation
Colorless glass, blown. Cut.

FS-G

209 a-c
Movement
H. 38.5 cm, D. 15.7 cm
Date: 1977
Colorless shading to opalescent
glass, blown. Enameled.

FS-G, RL, WS, PS

210
Bowl with Stem
H. 10.1 cm, D. 10.2 cm
Date: 1977
Signature: S/77
Colorless glass with opaque white
cane decoration. Lampwork.

WS, PS

Schaffer
Federal Republic of Germany

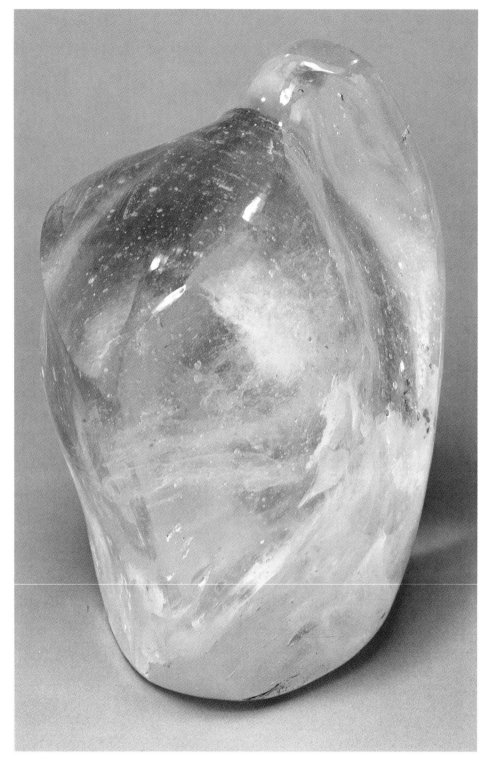

211
**Glass Sculpture Cut from
the Broken Piece**
H. 22.5 cm, W. 24.4 cm,
Depth 16.3 cm
Date: August 1977
Edition: 1/1
Pale aqua tinted bubbly glass, cast.
Cut.

FS-G

212
Cast Bowl with Inlaid
Enamel Colors
H. 8 cm, D. 50.3 cm
Date: February 1978
Signature: B. Schagemann/1978
Colorless glass with colored
decoration, cast. Enameled.

RL

Schmidt
United States

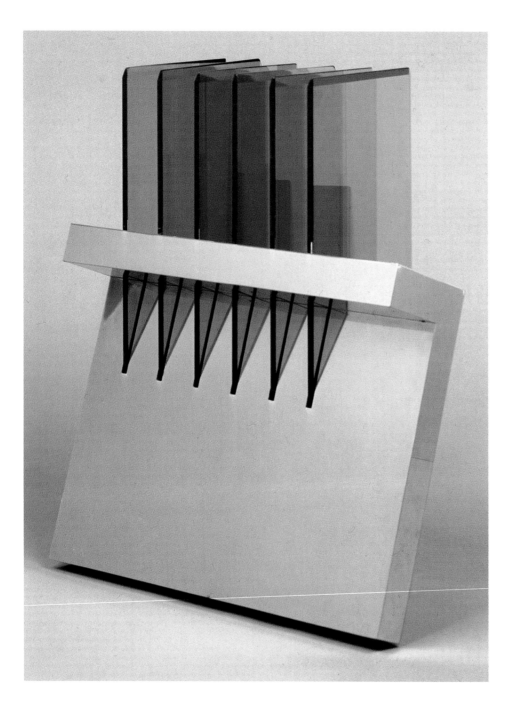

213
Elsix
H. 45 cm, W. 47.9 cm
Date: November 1976
Gray tinted plate glass sheets, cut.
Inserted into metal base.

PS

214
Corona Bowl
H. 5.9 cm, D. 38.6 cm
Date: February 1977
Signature: Steuben
Company: Steuben Glass
Colorless lead glass, blown.

RL

Sealine
United States

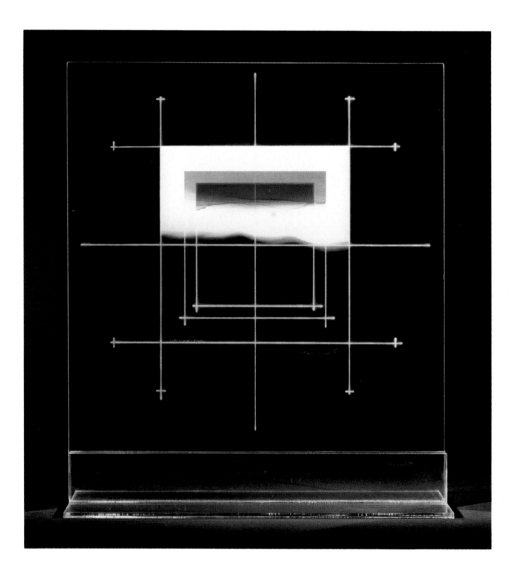

215
Bedrock Piece
H. (with base) 46.2 cm, W. 40.6 cm
Date: August 1978
Signature: Bedrock Piece/August
1978/Eric Sealine
Plate glass. Enameled, acid-
etched.

PS

216▶
Untitled
H. (with base) 103 cm, W. 56.5 cm
Date: February 1978
Signature: Seide/78
Colored glass, blown. Tubes filled
with neon, argon, and mercury
gas; electric discharge.

PS

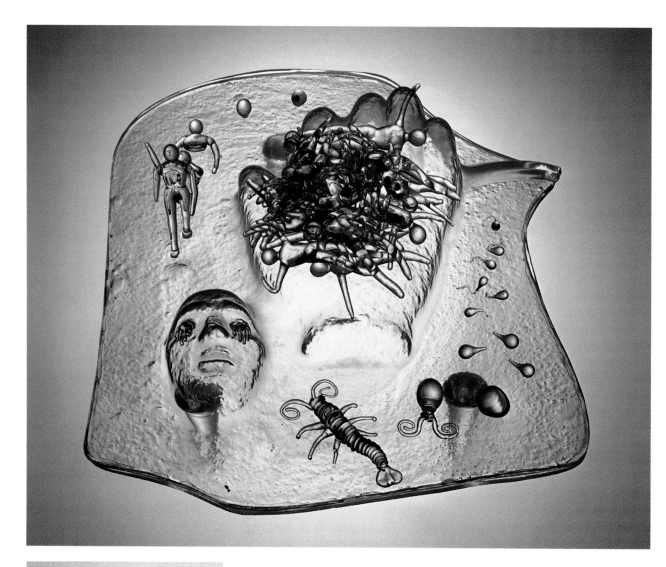

217
Staub
H. 15.7 cm, W. 37 cm,
Depth 45.1 cm
Date: 1977
Signature: Th. g. Sellner/Th. G.
Sellner 77
Colorless glass, sagged.
Lampwork.

WS

218
Sehnsucht
H. 22.8 cm, D. 19 cm
Date: 1977
Signature: Th. g. Sellner 77
Colorless glass. Lampwork.

FS-G, WS, PS

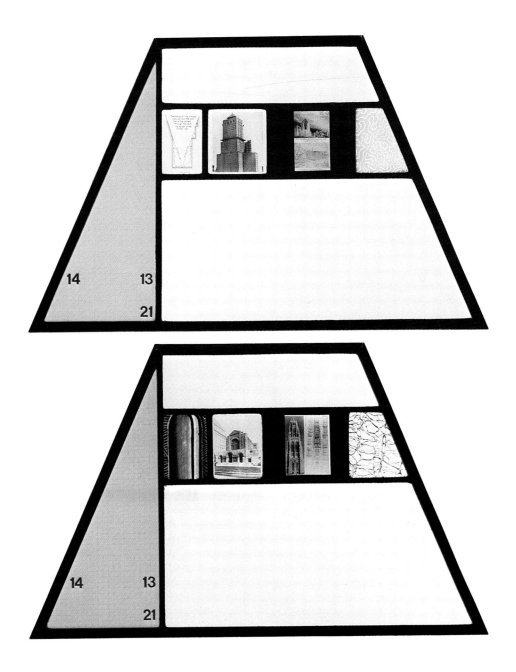

219 a-b
New York Windows #1
and #2
H. (of a) 34.6 cm, W. 55.5 cm
Date: 1976-1977
Signature: R SEWELL BETHANIA
77 (on each)
Flat glass with photoemulsions.
Some parts etched or enameled.
Leaded.

RL, PS

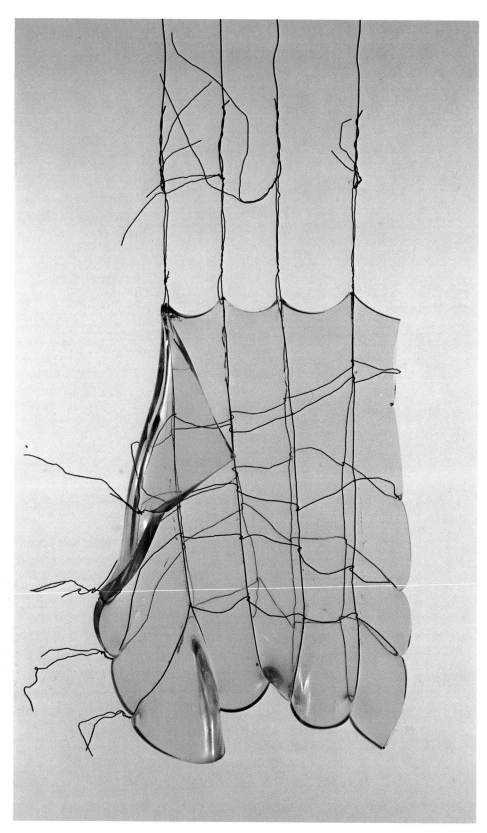

220
Hanging Series #15
H. 43.2 cm, W. 30.3 cm
Date: 1977
Signature: Mary Shaffer 77
Plate glass bound by wires,
slumped.

FS-G, RL, WS, PS

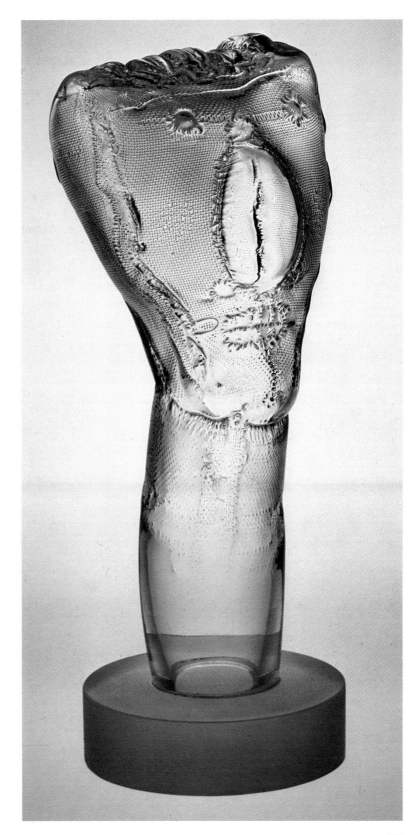

221
Head #4
H. 43.2 cm, W. 17.8 cm, D. 16.4 cm
Date: November 1977
Signature: Monogram 77
Colorless glass blown into sewn
copper mesh; mesh then
removed.

PS

222 a-f
New Mexico Goblets
H. (tallest) 24.3 cm, D. 7.2 cm
Date: January 1978
Signature: Simpson/78
Amethyst tinted glass with
blue/gray decoration, cased with
colorless glass, blown.

PS

223 a-c
Three Bottles
H. (tallest) 38 cm, W. 18 cm,
Depth 7.3 cm
Date: 1977
Signature: R. Sinnemark/BODA
1977
Company: Kosta Boda AB
Colorless glass with blue and red
enamel stoppers, blown-molded.
Etched.

RL, WS, PS

Šotola
Czechoslovakia

224
Colored Vase I
H. 29.8 cm, W. 21.5 cm,
Depth 10.2 cm
Date: February 1978
Blue and green tinted glass and
colorless glass, blown. Cut and
enameled.

PS

225
Colored Bowl IV
H. 4.5 cm, D. 34.7 cm
Date: January 1978
Colorless glass with multiple
colored layers, blown. Cut.

PS

226
Flow Gate
H. 27.2 cm, W. 68.5 cm,
Depth 43.2 cm
Date: 1976
Signature: Mark Stanley/1976
Broken plate glass, fused in
plaster forms. Neon loop. Black
glass base.

PS

Steuben Glass
United States

227
Paired Hearts
H. (tallest) 9.8 cm, W. 8.3 cm
Date: July 1977
Designer: James Carpenter
Colorless glass, pressed. Cut and
polished.

FS-G

228
Oriental Bowl
H. 17.7 cm, D. 31.4 cm
Date: July 1977
Designer: James Carpenter
Colorless glass, blown.

RL, PS

214

229
Votiv I
H. 61.7 cm, W. 51.2 cm
Date: 1978
Work done at the Studio of Franz
Mayer and Company, Munich.
Gray and colored glass. Some
parts acid-etched. Leaded.

PS

Stuhl
United States

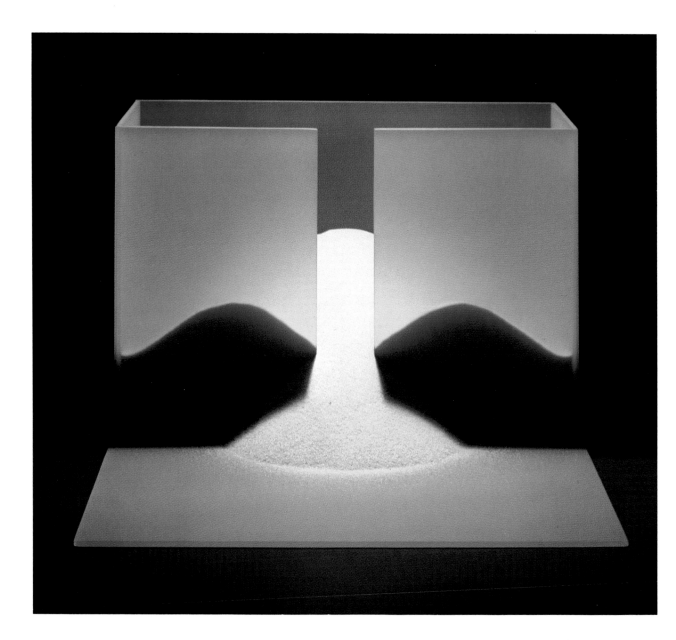

230
Containment-Escape
H. 25.8 cm, W. 40.5 cm
Date: March 1978 (ⓒ 1978)
Signature: Michelle Hope Stuhl
Plate glass. Sandblasted. Silica
sand.

FS-G, WS, PS

Šuhájek
Czechoslovakia

▲
231
Sculpture I
H. 51.2 cm, D. 16.6 cm
Date: January 1978
Signature: Jiří Šuhájek/78
Colorless glass with applied blue
tinted decoration, blown.

PS

232
Sculpture II
H. 50.7 cm, W. 32.5 cm
Date: January 1978
Signature: JIŘÍ Šuhájek/78
Colorless and blue tinted glass,
blown.

PS

Susquehanna Glass Company
United States

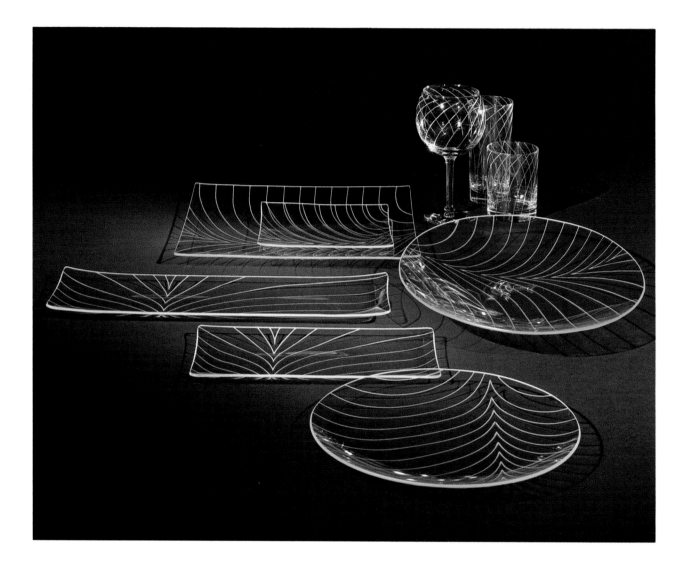

233 a-i
Designer Collection—
Windswept Pattern
H. (tallest) 19.6 cm, D. 11.1 cm
Date: Designed May 1977
Designer: William J. Kolano of
Irene Pasinski Associates
Colorless glass; the drinking ves-
sels machine blown. Stone wheel
cut.

FS-G, RL, WS, PS

234
On-the-Rocks
H. 9 cm, W. 8.1 cm,
Depth 8.1 cm

235
Highball
H. 12.1 cm, W. 7.7 cm,
Depth 7.7 cm

236
Schnaps
H. 9.1 cm, W. 5.7 cm,
Depth 5.7 cm

Company: Sasaki Glass Co., Ltd.
Date: February 1978
Colorless glass, mold-blown. Cut.

RL, PS

237
Sunrise
H. 15.3 cm, D. 10.2 cm
Date: November 1977
Colorless glass, cast and pulled.

FS-G, WS

238
Goblet
H. 16 cm, D. 10.7 cm
Date: 1976
Signature: Inkeri Toikka Nuu-
täjarvi Notsjo
Company: Nuutajärvi Glass
Opalescent and colorless glass,
blown.

FS-G

Torres Esteban
Spain

239
Volumenes
H. 34 cm, Depth 36.5 cm
Date: October 1976
Signature: Monogram 76
Pale green tinted flat glass. Laminated, cut, fractured.

PS

240
Egg II
H. 50 cm, W. 70 cm
Date: January 1978
Signature: Touskova 78
Cobalt blue tinted glass, blown
into plaster mold.

RL, PS

241
Piecrust Series
H. 6.9 cm, D. 30.1 cm
Date: March 1978
Signature: KARLA TRINKLEY/78
Colorless glass, slumped into
plaster mold. Sandblasted.

RL

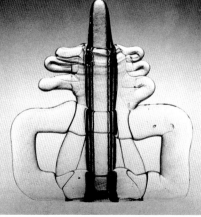

242
Captivity Unik 3476
H. 20.6 cm, W. 24.8 cm
Date: March 21, 1978
Signature: Ⓚ/KOSTA/UNIK
3476/B. VALLIEN
Company: Kosta Boda AB
Colorless and colored glass,
blown. Iridescent surfaces.
Sandblasted.

WS, PS

243 ▶
Cast Vase Atelje 191
H. 45 cm, W. 42.6 cm
Date: 1975
Signature: Boda Atelje 191 B. Val-
lien; Handmade/Kosta/Sweden
(on paper label)
Company: Kosta Boda AB
Colorless glass, free-cast.

WS, PS

Vallien
Sweden

244
Trumpet Blower
H. 47.1 cm, W. 45.1 cm
Date: January 3, 1977
Signature: BODA ATELJE 344/B.
Vallien
Company: Kosta Boda AB
Colorless glass, sandcast.

RL, WS, PS

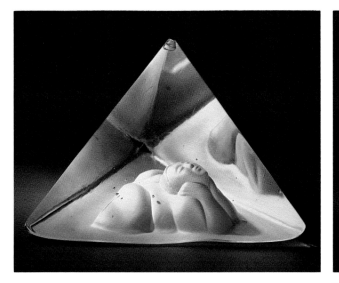

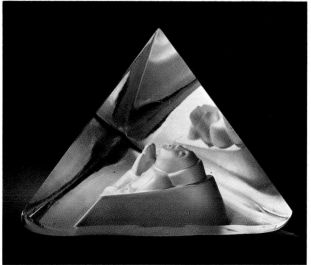

245 a-c
Chessmen:
King, Horse, Runner
H. (of a) 23.5 cm, W. 38.2 cm
Date: March 1978
Signature: B.V.L./V.S.L./m/march
78/1/10
Designer: Bert Van Loo
Edition: 1/10
Colorless glass, cast and cut.

RL, PS

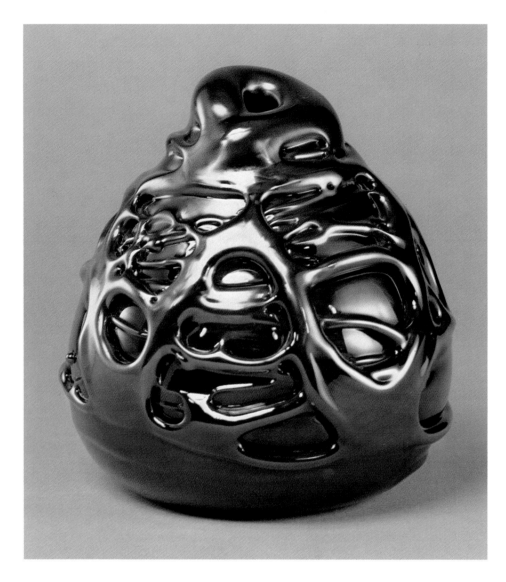

246
Vase I
H. 16.5 cm, D. 16.1 cm
Date: October 1977
Signature: V588 p Mark Vance
Oct. 1977
Amethyst tinted glass, blown.
Trailed decoration. Fumed.

WS

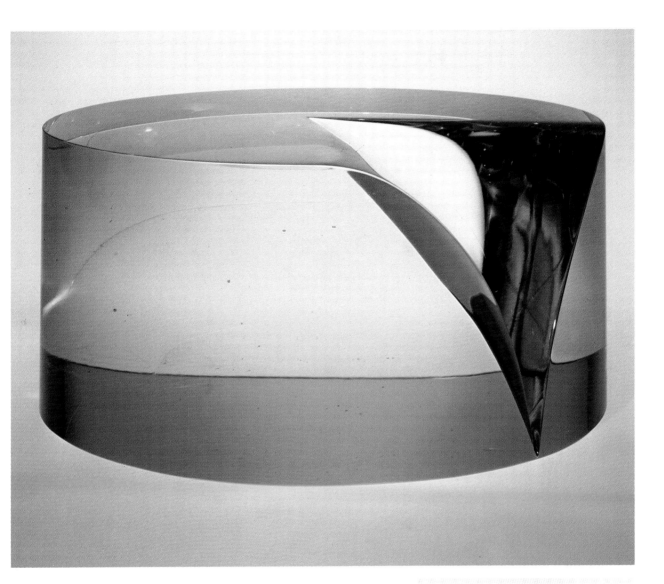

247
Cylinder
H. 12.3 cm, D. 26 cm
Date: February 1978
Signature: Aleš Vašíček 77
Colorless glass. Cut and polished.

FS-G, WS, PS

248 a-b
Cut Prisms
H. 26.4 cm, W. 21.8 cm
Date: March 1977
Signature: 1977 ALEŠ VAŠÍČEK
Colorless glass. Cut and polished.
Two parts.

FS-G, WS

Vennola
Finland

249 a-e
Punch Bowl with Ladle
and Mugs
H. (bowl) 12.9 cm, D. 24 cm
Date: February 1978
Signature: Bowl: i/Made in
Finland (on triangular label)
Company: Iittala Glassworks
Colorless glass, mold-blown.
Metal handles.

FS-G, PS

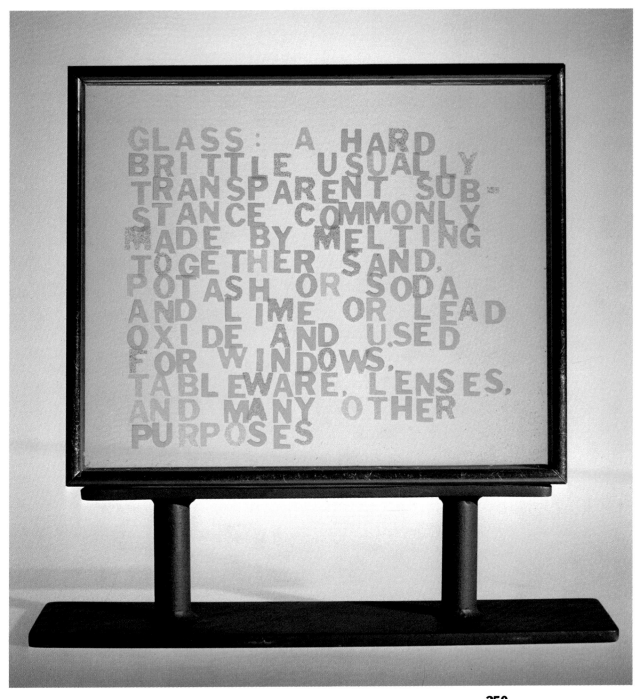

250
"...And Many Other Purposes"
H. 29.2 cm, W. 30.8 cm
Date: February 1978
Signature: Robert Vesely
Several layers of colorless plate glass. Hand-stenciled, sand-blasted.

RL

Vida
Hungary

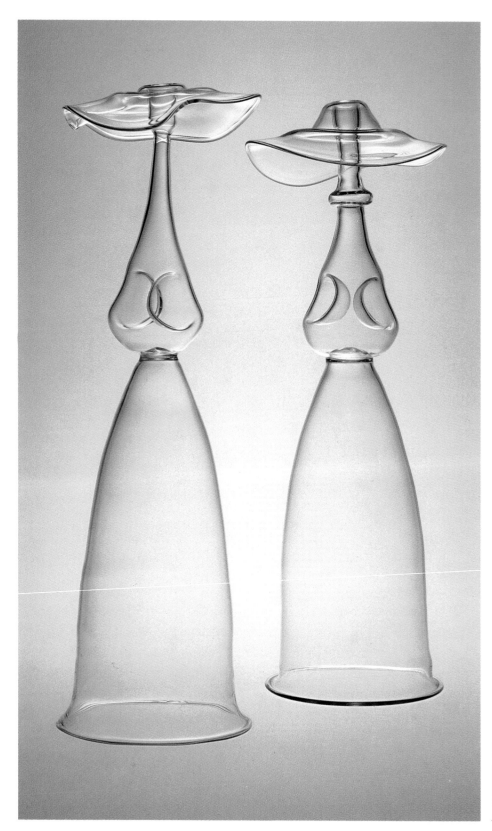

251a-b
Two Crystal Figures
H. 43.9 cm, D. 13.7 cm
Date: 1978
Signature: Monogram
Colorless glass. Lampwork.

RL, PS

252
Untitled
H. 9.1 cm, W. 8.7 cm,
Depth 4.4 cm
Date: December 1977
Signature: Syl Vigiletti 1977
Silver veiling glass, multiple
gathers, blown.

WS

Vignelli Associates
United States

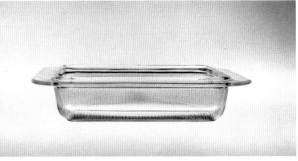

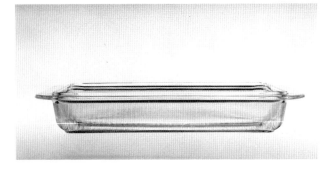

253	254
255	257
256	

253
**Three Quart Casserole
with Au Gratin Cover**
H. 14.2 cm, D. 29.1 cm
Date: 1977
Signature: HELLER OVEN/MICRO-
WAVE BAKEWARE DESIGN BY
L&M VIGNELLI MADE IN USA 20
Designers: Lella and Massimo
Vignelli
Colorless glass, pressed.

PS

254
**Two Quart Casserole
with Au Gratin Cover**
H. 14 cm, D. 24.8 cm
Date: 1977

FS-G

255
Deep Loaf/Paté Pan
H. 7.7 cm, W. 17 cm,
Depth 24.5 cm
Date: 1975

FS-G

256
2-1/2 Quart Lasagna Dish
H. 5.7 cm, W. 28.2 cm,
Depth 38.2 cm
Date: 1975

FS-G

257
8″ Square Cake/Bake Dish
H. 5.4 cm, W. 26.5 cm,
Depth 26.4 cm
Date: 1975

FS-G

258
Smoked Bowl
H. 9.3 cm, D. 29 cm
Date: February 1978
Gray tinted glass. Cut, sand-
blasted, polished.

FS-G, RL, WS, PS

Vízner
Czechoslovakia

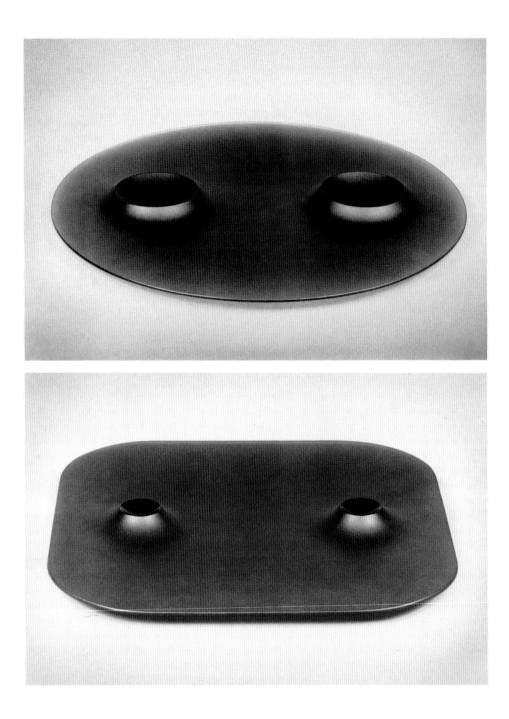

259
Green Plate
D. 45.4 cm
Date: March 1978
Green tinted glass. Cut, sand-
blasted, polished.

PS

260
Blue Plate
W. 38.2 cm, D. 38.1 cm
Date: October 1977
Blue tinted glass. Cut, sand-
blasted, polished.

PS

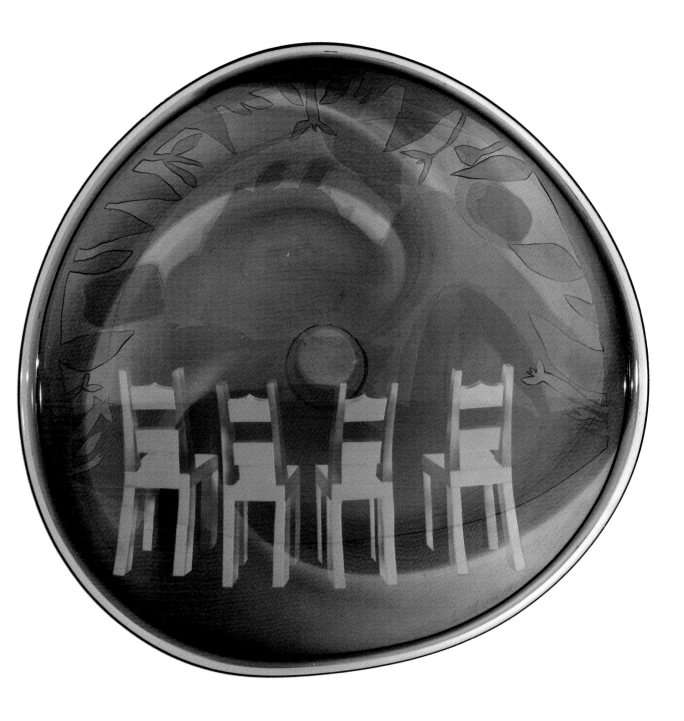

261
Plate Scenery
H. 6 cm, D. 50.4 cm
Date: 1978
Signature: Ann Wärff KOSTA 1978
Company: Kosta Boda AB
Several layers of cased glass,
blown. Acid-etched, sandblasted.

RL, PS

262
Bowl Life
H. 9.8 cm, D. 20.9 cm
Date: 1978
Signature: "BOWL-LIFE" Ann
Wärff KOSTA 78
Company: Kosta Boda AB
Several layers of cased glass,
blown. Acid-etched, sandblasted.

RL

263
Glass
H. 60.1 cm, W. 50.2 cm
Date: 1977
Signature: Ann Wärff KOSTA 1977
Company: Kosta Boda AB
Colorless sheet glass. Sand-
blasted, mirrored, with added
colorless glass decoration.

FS-G, RL, PS

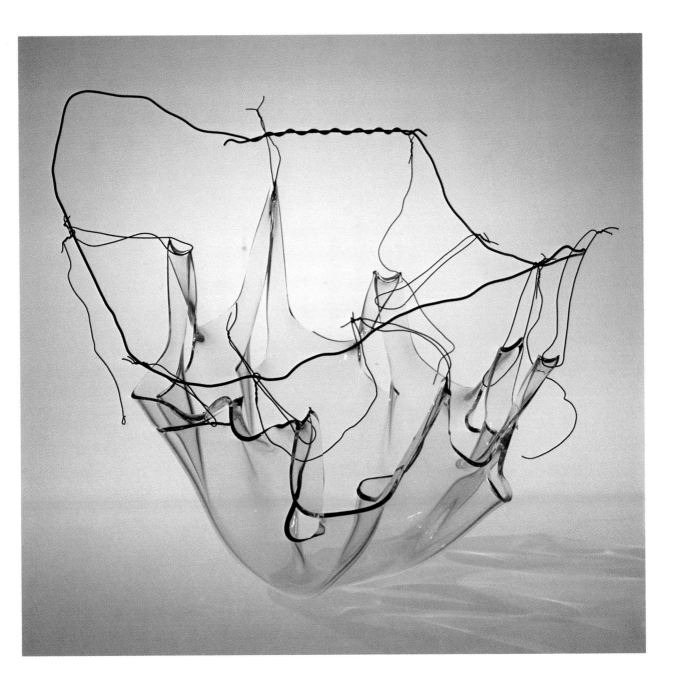

264
Bowl #2
H. 26.6 cm, W. 22.6 cm
Date: March 1978
Nearly colorless glass; sand-
blasted holes with drawn wire.
Sagged.

FS-G, WS

265
Double Cross
H. 8.1 cm, W. 19.6 cm,
Depth 19.5 cm
Date: March 1978
Light green tinted glass, cast. Cut
and polished.

PS

240

266
Robot
H. 16.7 cm, W. 19.6 cm
Date: September 1976
Amethyst tinted glass. Lampwork.

WS

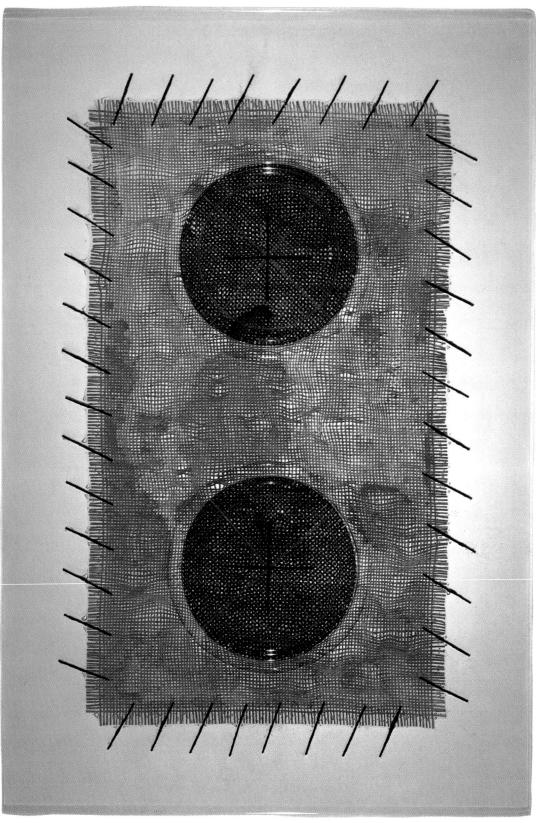

◄ **267**
Stourbridge Series #32
H. 56.1 cm, W. 38.4 cm
Date: November 1976
Signature: Willard 77
Flat glass and woven fiberglass,
fused.

PS

268
Untitled
H. 37.9 cm, W. 35.4 cm
Date: 1975
Signature: WILLET/ STAINED
GLASS CO/FARBIGEM
Colorless and colored sheet glass,
laminated. Wooden base.

FS-G, RL

Wlodarczyk-Puchała
Poland

269
Gracja I
H. 22 cm, D. 20.9 cm
Date: 1977
Signature: RWP
Colorless glass, blown. Cut.

PS

244

270
Seaweed II
H. 14.6 cm, D. 16.5 cm
Date: November 1977
Signature: A. Wolowska
Several layers of colored glass
decoration, blown.

RL

Zaglauer
Federal Republic of Germany

271
Lead Crystal Vase
H. 13.3 cm, D. 12.7
Date: May 17, 1977
Signature: BLEIKRISTAL/
BAVARIA/GERMANY
(on paper label)
Company: Nachtmann, KG, F.X.
Colorless glass with white and
gray internal decoration, blown.

RL

272
Painted Vase
H. 53.8 cm, W. 30.8 cm,
Depth 22.6 cm
Date: November 1977
Signature: ZERTOVA
Colorless, amber, and green
tinted glass, blown. Enameled.

WS

Zoritchak
Czechoslovakia (working in France)

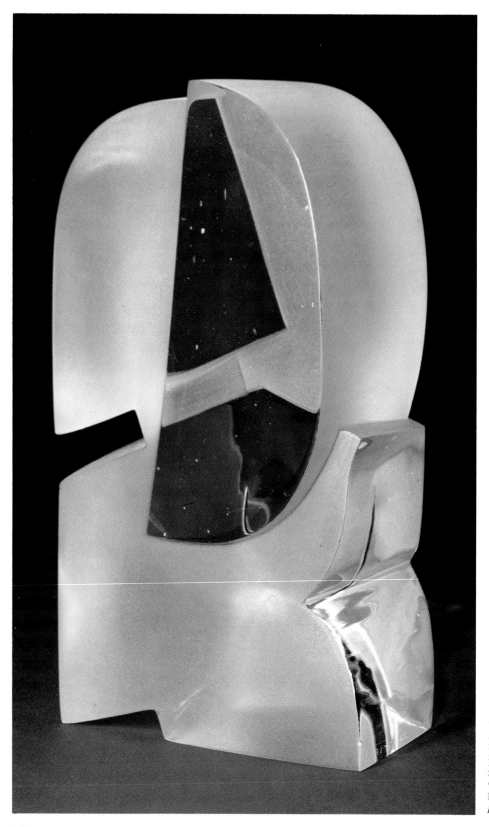

273
Equilibre
H. 26.1 cm, W. 16.1 cm,
Depth 8.4 cm
Date: 1976
Signature: ZORITCHAK 1978
Colorless glass, cast. Cut and
polished.

FS-G

Glassmakers, Designers, and Companies

Space restrictions have required editing the biographical information about education, exhibitions, and publications. The latter two items are intended, therefore, only as references to sources of more information about the artist/company involved.

Biographical details about many of the participants in *New Glass* may be obtained from: Geoffrey Beard, *International Modern Glass;* Ray and Lee Grover, *Contemporary Art Glass,* and the following exhibition catalogs: *American Glass Now* (Toledo); *Coburger Glaspreis* (Coburg); *Glass '78 in Japan* (Tokyo); and *Modernes Glas* (Frankfurt). See complete citations in the bibliography. Additional information about glassmaking companies is provided in *The Glass Industry Directory Issue 1979,* Vol. 59, No. 10, 1979.

Jan Adam
Czechoslovakia
Ovenecká 32
1700 00 Praha 7-Letná
Czechoslovakia
Born May 6, 1948

Jan Adam is a free-lance glass designer. Education: High School, Liberec, 1963-1967; Academy of Applied Arts, Prague 1968-1974. Selected Major Exhibitions: International Fair of Arts and Handicrafts, Munich, 1978. Publications: *Contemporary Glass in Czechoslovakia,* Prague, 1977 (exhibition catalog).

Blanka Adensamová
Czechoslovakia
Gorazdova 20
120 00 Praha 2, Vinohrady
Czechoslovakia
Born November 24, 1948

Blanka Adensamová is a free-lance glass designer. Education: High School of Applied Arts in Glass, Železný Brod 1967-1970; Academy of Applied Arts, Prague 1970-1976. Selected Major Exhibitions: *Glass from Czechoslovakia,* Moscow, 1974 and Leningrad, 1975.

Anchor Hocking
Corporation
Lancaster, Ohio 43130
U.S.A.

Anchor Hocking was founded in 1904 and employs 17,000. The company specializes in the production of glass, ceramic, and plastic containers and tableware.

Tom Armbruster
United States
1671 Franklin Avenue, Apt. 216
Kent, Ohio 44240
U.S.A.
Born June 23, 1953

Tom Armbruster is a Teaching Assistant at Kent State University. Education: Kent State University, B.F.A.

Herbert Babcock
United States
716 Coughlan
Auburn Heights, Michigan 48057
U.S.A.
Born June 11, 1946

Herbert Babcock is an Assistant Professor at the College of Art and Design, Detroit, Michigan. Education: Cleveland Institute of Art 1964-1969; The Toledo Museum of Art Glass Studio 1970; Cranbrook Academy of Art 1971-1973. Selected Major Exhibitions: *Contemporary Art Glass,* New York, 1976; *Glass America, 1978,* New York, 1978. Publications: *Your Portable Museum.* American Crafts Council, 1978.

Compagnie des
Cristalleries
de Baccarat
54120 Nancy
France

Baccarat was founded in 1764 and presently employs 1,070 individuals. Prominent for its production of paperweights in the midnineteenth century, the factory today produces a wide range of objects including table glasses and glass sculptures, vases and decorative pieces.

Monica Backström
Sweden
Boda Bruks AB
360 65 Boda Glasbruk
Sweden
Born May 20, 1939

Monica Backström has designed for Boda since 1965. Education: Konstfackskolan in Stockholm 1959-1964. Publications: *Form,* No. 9, 1965, pp. 608-609.

Dan Băncilá
Romania
Iovita Street, 27
Sector 6, Bucarest-7000
Romania
Born October 7, 1943

Dan Băncilá has worked as a glass artist since 1971. Education: Plastic Art Institute, Nicolae Grigorescu, Bucharest, 1964-1970. Selected Major Exhibitions: *Coburger Glaspreis,* Coburg, 1977. Publications: Dan Băncilá, Sticla, Galeria Simeza 1975 (exhibition catalog).

VETRERIA IN F.TA VENIER 48 MURANO ITALIA

Alfredo Barbini
Italy
Calle dell'artigiano II
Murano
Italy

Barbini was founded in 1950 and employs 22 people.

Paula Bartron
United States
(working in Sweden)
Glas, Box 27117
10252 Stockholm
Sweden
Born December 3, 1946

Paula Bartron is presently a lecturer in glass at the Konstfackskolan, Stockholm, Sweden. Education: College of San Mateo, California, A.A., 1967; University of California, Berkeley, A.B., 1970, M.A., 1972; Nybro Glasskolan, Orrefors, Sweden, 1973-1974. Selected Major Exhibitions: *American Glass Now,* Toledo, 1972; *Coburger Glaspreis,* Coburg, 1977.

Hans Theodor Baumann
Federal Republic of
Germany
7860 Schopfheim
Frieseneggerweg 7/Postfach 1269
Federal Republic of Germany
Born October 27, 1924

Hans Baumann has managed an independent design studio since 1950. Education: Kunstgewerbeschule, Basel, Switzerland, 1945-1950. Selected Major Exhibitions: *Milan Triennale,* 1954, 1957; *Coburger Glaspreis,* Coburg, 1977. Publications: *Idea,* International Advertising Art, Japan Publications Trading Co. Ltd., vol. 71/7, 1971, pp. 80 ff.

Hartmut Bechmann
German Democratic
Republic
6422 Ernstthal Forstweg 22
German Democratic Republic
Born June 1, 1939

Hartmut Bechmann is a free-lance glass artist. Education: Scheeburg College of Art, 1970-1973.

Howard Ben Tré
United States
158 Miller Avenue
Providence, Rhode Island 02905
U.S.A.
Born May 13, 1949

Howard Ben Tré is a graduate student at the Rhode Island School of Design. Education: Portland State University, B.S., 1978. Publications: The Corning Museum of Glass, *Contemporary Glass 1977,* Corning, 1978.

Karl R. Berg
Federal Republic of
Germany
Theresienstr. 140
D-8000, München 2
Federal Republic of Germany
Born January 29, 1943

Karl Berg is a glass designer. Education: Glasfachschule, Zwiesel; Kunstakademie, Munich. Selected Major Exhibitions: *Coburger Glaspreis,* Coburg 1977; Museum für Kunst und Gewerbe, Hamburg, 1978.

Rick Bernstein
United States
125 Montague Road
Amherst, Massachusetts 01002
U.S.A.
Born October 29, 1952

Rick Bernstein is a glassworker. Education: University of Massachusetts, B.A.; Tyler School of Art, M.F.A. Selected Major Exhibitions: *Pilchuck Glass Invitational,* Modern Art Pavilion, Seattle, 1976; *Fragile Art '77,* Glassmasters Gallery, New York, 1978.

William Bernstein
United States
Box 73AA, Rt. 5
Burnsville, North Carolina 28714
U.S.A.
Born December 3, 1945

William Bernstein has been an active studio glass artist since 1968; from 1968-1970 he was Craftsman-in-residence at the Penland School of Crafts. Education: Philadelphia College of Art, B.F.A., 1968. Selected Major Exhibitions: *American Glass Now,* Toledo, 1972; *North Carolina Glass, '78,* Cullowhee, North Carolina.

Heidi-Astrid Betz-Schlierer
Federal Republic of Germany
Volkartstr.43/VI, 8000, Munich 19
Federal Republic of Germany
Born November 3, 1938

Heide-Astrid Betz-Schlierer is a free-lance artist who has had her own atelier since 1968. Education: Academy of Arts, Florence; Academy of Arts, Munich. Selected Major Exhibitions: *Coburger Glaspreis,* Coburg, 1977. Publications: Hans Jebsen-Marwedel. *Glas in Kultur und Technik.* Selb: Verlag Aumann KG, 1976, pp. 185-186.

Jonathan Block
United States
910 West Hill
Champaign, Illinois 61820
U.S.A.
Born June 17, 1949

Jonathan Block teaches at Parkland College, Champaign, Illinois. Education: Philadelphia College of Art, B.S.; Kent State University, M.A.; Washington State University, M.F.A. Selected Major Exhibitions: *Contemporary Art Glass '76,* New York.

Zoltan Bohus
Hungary
Mártirok Útza 41
1024 Budapest
Hungary
Born December 21, 1941

Zoltan Bohus is a member of the Silicate Design Department, College of Applied Arts, Budapest. Education: College of Applied Arts, Budapest, 1966. Publications: Nagy Ildiko, "Bohus Zoltan plasztikái," *Müvészet,* 1977/5, pp. 18-21.

Arne Branzell
Sweden
Grimmereds By 31
42170 V: a Frölunda
Sweden
Born October 2, 1932

Arne Branzell is a practicing architect and designer who has designed objects for Kosta Boda in Sweden. Education: Gothenburg School of Design; Chalmers University of Technology.

Jaroslava Brychtová
Czechoslovakia
Brodec 645, 468 22 Železný Brod
Czechoslovakia
Born July 17, 1924

Jaroslava Brychtová has been a glass designer at the Želznobrodské sklo glassworks, Železný Brod, since 1950. Education: Academy of Applied Arts, Prague, 1944-1947; Academy of Fine Arts, Prague, 1947-1950. Selected Major Exhibitions: *Coburger Glaspreis,* Coburg, 1977.

John Burton
United States
RR 1, Box 288J
Kapaa, Kauai, Hawaii 96746
U.S.A.
Born May 8, 1894

John Burton is a free-lance glass artist and lecturer. Selected Major Exhibitions: *Glass 1959,* Corning. Publications: John Burton. *Glass: Philosophy and Method, Handblown, Sculptured, Colored.* Philadelphia: Chilton Book Company, 1967.

Cá D'Oro Ltda.
Av. João Pinheiro 1919
Caixa Posta 628-Pocos de Caldas
37700
Brasil

Cá D'Oro was founded February 26, 1965, and employs 46 people. Its productions include utilitarian wares and objects for decoration.

Diane H. Castellan
United States
12 Smoke Hill Drive
New Fairfield, Connecticut 06810
U.S.A.
Born May 26, 1955

Diane Castellan is a self-employed artist. Education: Cleveland Institute of Art, B.F.A., 1978. Selected Major Exhibitions: *Young Americans: Fiber / Wood / Plastic / Leather,* New York.

Dale Chihuly
United States
115 Williams Street
Providence, Rhode Island 02906
U.S.A.
Born September 20, 1941

Dale Chihuly is chairman of the Glass Department at Rhode Island School of Design and Educational Coordinator of the Pilchuck Art Center. Education: University of Washington, B.F.A., 1965; University of Wisconsin, M.S., 1967; Rhode Island School of Design, M.F.A., 1968. Selected Major Exhibitions: *Objects U.S.A.,* Washington, D.C., 1969; *American Glass Now,* Toledo, 1972; *Glaskunst der Gegenwart,* Kassel, 1977. Publications: Hall, Julie. *Tradition and Change.*

Dillon Clarke
England
69 Grasmere Road
London N.10
Great Britain
Born February 18, 1946

Dillon Clarke, a part-time lecturer at Middlesex Polytechnic, London, worked briefly at Dartington Glass in 1970; from 1970-1975 she was a member of the Glasshouse Workshop in Covent Garden. Education: Stoke-on-Trent College of Art 1962-1964; Hornsey College of Art 1964-1967; Royal College of Art 1967-1970. Selected Major Exhibitions: *Coburger Glaspreis,* Coburg, 1977. Publications: Geoffrey Beard, *International Modern Glass.* London: Barrie and Jenkins, 1976.

James Clarke
United States
2510 N. 47th Street
Boulder, Colorado 80301
U.S.A.
Born May 21, 1951

James Clarke is the owner/operator of Clarke Glass Studio. Education: University of Wisconsin, B.S., 1973; M.F.A., 1976.

Robert Cmarik
United States
4582 East Berwald Road
South Euclid, Ohio 44121
U.S.A.
Born December 23, 1954

Education: Cleveland State University, 1977.

Michael Cohn
United States
5998 Hollis Street
Emeryville, California 94608
U.S.A.
Born January 17, 1949

Michael Cohn owns a private studio and teaches glassblowing at California State University, San Francisco. Education: Long Beach City College; University of California, Berkeley. Selected Major Exhibitions: *American Glass Now,* Toledo, 1972; *Glaskunst der Gegenwart,* Kassel, 1977. Publications: Julie Hall. *Tradition and Change: The New American Craftsman.* New York: E.P. Dutton, 1977, p. 95.

Jamie L. Conover
United States
921 South Main Street
Phoenixville, Pennsylvania 19460
U.S.A.
Born July 7, 1954

Jamie Conover is currently working with a craftsman in fiberglass processes. Education: Pennsylvania State University, B.F.A., 1976; Tyler School of Art, M.F.A., 1978.

John Heald Cook
England
53 The Banks
Sileby, Leicestershire LE1 9BH
Great Britain
Born September 19, 1942

John Cook, now head of ceramics, silver, and glass studies at Leicester Polytechnic, was a visiting designer at Venini Glass, Murano, Italy (1969-1970), and chairman/founder member of British Artists in Glass. Education: School of Art, Preston 1960-1962; College of Art and Design, Leeds 1962-1965; Royal College of Art, London 1965-1968. Selected Major Exhibitions: *Coburger Glaspreis,* 1977. Publications: Geoffrey Beard, *International Modern Glass.*

Cowdy Glass Workshop
Limited
27 Culver Street
Newent, Gloucestershire GL18 1DB
England

Cowdy Glass was founded January 3, 1977, and employs five people. It specializes in the production of handmade, colored glass.

Gunnar Cyrén
Sweden
Domargränd 12
S-802 23 Gävle
Sweden
Born July 23, 1931

Gunnar Cyrén is a free-lance designer for A.B. Orrefors Glassbruk and has designed for Dansk Designs, Ltd. Education: Konstfackskolan, Stockholm.

Dan Dailey
United States
122 Market Street
Amesbury, Massachusetts 01913
U.S.A.
Born February 4, 1947

Dan Dailey, presently head of the Glass Department at Massachusetts College of Art, Boston, has been a guest designer for Fabrica Venini, Murano, Italy, and is currently designing for Cristallerie Daum, Nancy, France. Education: Philadelphia College of Art B.F.A.; Rhode Island School of Design M.F.A. Selected Major Exhibitions: *American Glass Now,* Toledo, 1972; *Glass America, 1978,* New York. Publications: Julie Hall, *Tradition and Change.* New York: E.P. Dutton, 1977.

Daum & Cie
41 rue de Paradis
75010 Paris
France

Daum was founded in 1875 and employs 220 people. It specializes in lead crystal and pâte-de-verre and decorative items such as lamp bases, clocks, and candlesticks.

William Dexter
United States
409 Bayview Drive
Clearwater, Florida 33516
U.S.A.
Born April 7, 1952

William Dexter, now a student at the Tyler School of Art, has been a Teaching Assistant at the Pilchuck Art Center, and the Haystack Mountain School of Crafts. Education: University of Miami; University of Wisconsin.

David Dowler
United States
120 East Third Street
Corning, New York 14830
U.S.A.
Born February 1, 1944

David Dowler is a designer for Steuben Glass. Education: Syracuse University, B.I.D., 1969.

Antonín Drobník
Czechoslovakia
Sporílov 654
468 22 Železný R Brod
Czechoslovakia
Born April 20, 1925

Antonín Drobník has been a glass designer at the Železnobroské Sklárny Glassworks since 1951. Education: High School of Applied Arts in Glass, Železný Brod 1940-1943; Academy of Applied Arts, Prague, 1943-1949. Selected Major Exhibitions: *Böhmisches Glas der Gegenwart,* Hamburg, 1973-1974.

Richard Duggan
United States
396-49th Street
Oakland, California 94609
U.S.A.
Born July 15, 1952

Richard Duggan is a graduate student at the California College of Arts and Crafts. Education: Pratt Institute; Massachusetts College of Art B.F.A. Center for Advanced Visual Studies, M.I.T.; Selected Major Exhibitions: New York Experimental Glass Workshop, 1978.

Udo Edelmann
Federal Republic of Germany
Wiesenstr. 17, 5010 Bergheim
Federal Republic of Germany
Born October 6, 1938

Udo Edelmann is technical manager of a German glass factory. Education: Glasfachschule, Rheinbach. Selected Major Exhibitions: *Coburger Glaspreis,* Coburg, 1977.

Erwin Eisch
Federal Republic of
Germany
D-8371 Frauenau, Bayer. Wald
Federal Republic of Germany
Born April 18, 1927

Erwin Eisch works independently at his Frauenau studio and also designs for the family factory, Valentin Eisch K.G. Education: Akademie der Bildenden Künste, München, 1946-1949; Fachschule Zwiesel, 1949-1950. Selected Major Exhibitions: *Glas heute, Kunst oder Handwerk?*, Zurich, 1972, *Modernes Glas,* Frankfurt, 1976; *Coburger Glaspreis,* Coburg, 1977; *Glaskunst der Gegenwart,* Kassel, 1977. Publications: H. Spielmann. *Erwin Eisch, Narziss-ein-Interieur.* Hamburg, 1971.

Margarete Eisch
Federal Republic of
Germany
D-8371 Frauenau, Bayer. Wald
Federal Republic of Germany
Born February 15, 1937

Margarete Eisch works as a glass artist at Frauenau. Education: Fine Art School, Munich. Selected Major Exhibitions: *Modernes Glas,* Frankfurt, 1976; *Coburger Glaspreiz,* Coburg, 1977.

Michael D. Esson
England (working in
Australia)
1/88 Brighton Boulevarde
North Bondi, N.S.W., Australia
Born March 19, 1950

Michael Esson is presently a lecturer in sculpture at Alexander Mackie C.A.E., Sydney; he has worked for Perthshire Paperweights, Ltd., Scotland, and Optical Ltd., London. Education: Edinburgh College of Art; Royal College of Art, London. Publications: *British Crafts Magazine,* Sept./October 1977, p. 32.

Ray Flavell
England
December, Clovelly Road
Hindhead, Surrey GU26 6QD
England
Born March 31, 1944

Ray Flavell is at present a lecturer in glass at West Surrey College of Art and Design and has designed for Stevens and Williams Ltd. Education: Wolverhampton College of Art; Royal College of Art, London. Selected Major Exhibitions: *Modernes Glass,* Frankfurt, 1976; *Coburger Glaspreis,* Coburg, 1977.

Ulla Forsell
Sweden
Västmannagatan 78
S-113 26 Stockholm
Sweden
Born February 29, 1944

Ulla Forsell is an independent glass artist. Education: Konstfackskolan, Stockholm 1966-1971; Glasskolan, Orrefors, 1971-1973; Rietveld Akademie, Amsterdam, 1973. Selected Major Exhibitions: *Coburger Glaspreis,* Coburg, 1977.

Hans Godo Fräbel
United States
695 Antone Street N.W.
Atlanta, Georgia 30318
U.S.A.
Born June 9, 1941

Hans Fräbel, the principal artist at the Fräbel Studio, has worked as a scientific glassblower at Georgia Institute of Technology and the Jena Glaswerke in Mainz, West Germany. Education: Georgia State University. Selected Major Exhibitions: *Glass America, 1978,* New York.

Saburo Funakoshi
Japan
No. 2-8-3 Kyobashi
Chuo-ku, Tokyo
Japan
Born March 27, 1931

Mr. Funakoshi is director of Hoya Corporation, Musashi Plant, Design Department. Education: Tokyo University of Fine Arts. Selected Major Exhibitions: *Glass 78 in Japan,* Odakyu Department Store, Tokyo 1978.

Klaus Geller
Federal Republic of
Germany
Rubensstr. 25/27, D-5000
Cologne 1
Federal Republic of Germany
Born April 6, 1944

Klaus Geller, a self-employed glass artist, has owned his own atelier since 1970. Education: Study of glass/painting 1958-1961. Selected Major Exhibitions: *Internationaler Kunstmarkt,* Düsseldorf, 1976.

Dudley F. Giberson
United States
Box 202, Joppa Road
Warner, New Hampshire 03278
U.S.A.
Born December 14, 1942

Dudley Giberson is a self-employed artist. Education: Rhode Island School of Design, B.F.A., 1967.

Marianne Gille
Sweden
Riddargatan 41
114 57 Stockholm
Sweden
Born November 28, 1944

Marianne Gille is a free-lance designer and assistant teacher at the Konstfackskolan, Stockholm. Education: Konstfackskolan, Stockholm, 1978.

John D. Gilmor
United States
Drawer H, Route 82
Pine Plains, New York 12567
U.S.A.
Born June 6, 1950

John Gilmor is the owner of the Gilmor Glass Works. Education: Denison University, B.F.A.; Southern Illinois University, M.F.A.

Gral-Glashütte GmbH
Durnau, Postfach 1124
D-7320 Göppingen
Federal Republic of Germany

Gral-Glashütte was founded in 1946 and employs 300 people. It specializes in stemware, glass sculptures, and replicas of antique glassware.

J.R. Grossman
United States
126 Berkley
Dearborn, Michigan 48124
U.S.A.

Education: Illinois State University, B.S.

Henry Halem
United States
429 Carthage Avenue
Kent, Ohio 44240
U.S.A.
Born May 5, 1938

Henry Halem is Associate Professor of Art in glass at Kent State University. He is past President of the Glass Art Society and a member of its Board of Directors. Education: Rhode Island School of Design, B.F.A.; George Washington University, M.F.A. Selected Major Exhibitions: *American Glass Now,* Toledo, 1972; *International Glass Sculpture,* Miami, 1973; *Glass America, 1978,* New York, 1978.

Audrey Handler
United States
105 South Rock Road
Madison, Wisconsin 53705
U.S.A.
Born December 9, 1934

Audrey Handler has operated a private glassblowing studio since 1971; she teaches part time at Madison Area Technical College and is currently secretary of the Glass Arts Society. Education: Tyler School of Art, 1952-1954; Boston University School of Fine Arts, B.F.A., 1956; University of Wisconsin, M.S., 1967; M.F.A., 1970. Selected Major Exhibitions: *American Glass Now,* Toledo, 1972.

Jiří Harcuba
Czechoslovakia
Janouškova 1
162 00 Praha 6, Dejvice
Czechoslovakia
Born December 6, 1928

Jiří Harcuba is a glass designer. Education: High School of Applied Arts, Nový Bor, 1945-1947; Academy of Applied Arts, Prague, 1949-1954. Selected Major Exhibitions: *Bohemian Glass,* Victoria and Albert Museum, London, 1965; *Coburger Glaspreis,* Coburg, 1977.

James R. Harmon
United States
21 Bernon Street
Providence, Rhode Island 02908
U.S.A.
Born November 18, 1952

James Harmon is a glass designer-fabricator. Education: Rhode Island School of Design, B.F.A., 1975; Illinois State University, M.F.A., 1978; Selected Major Exhibitions: *Young Americans: Clay/Glass,* Museum of Contemporary Crafts, New York, 1978; *Glass America,* 1978.

Richard Spencer Harned
United States
Spring Dell Lane
Chapel Hill, North Carolina
27514
U.S.A.
Born May 3, 1951

Richard Harned is Assistant Professor of Sculpture at the University of Tennessee, Knoxville; from 1973 to 1975 he was the owner/operator of a sculpture studio and glassworking business. Education: Rhode Island School of Design. Publications: *Glass Art Magazine,* October 1976, Vol. 4, No. 7, p. 17.

Willem Heesen
Netherlands
Industrieweg 1 4143 MP
Leerdam
Netherlands
Born February 26, 1925

Willem Heesen, chief Designer at Royal Leerdam since 1967, is owner of the glass studio "Oude Horn," Acquoy. Education: Glasschool Leerdam Vrije Academie voor Beeldende Kunsten, Den Haag, Amsterdam. Selected Major Exhibitions: *Glass 1959,* Corning; *Glas heute, Kunst oder Handwerk?,* Zurich, 1972. *Modernes Glas,* Frankfurt, 1976; *Coburger Glaspreis,* Coburg, 1977. *Publications: R. Stennett-Willson. The Beauty of Modern Glass.* London: Studio Limited, 1958, p. 81.

Lars Hellsten
Sweden
Heddamåla 36053 Skruv
Sweden
Born July 18, 1933

Lars Hellsten is an independent glassworker who has designed for Skrufs Glasbruk and Orrefors Glasbruk. Education: Konstfackskolan, Stockholm, 1957-1963. Selected Major Exhibitions: *L'Art des Maitres Verriers,* Brussels, 1974; *Adventure in Swedish Glass,* Australia, 1975-1976; *Modernes Glass,* Frankfurt, 1976. Publications: Geoffrey Beard. *International Modern Glass.* London: Barrie and Jenkins, 1976, p. 36.

Eric Hilton
Scotland (working in USA)
Box 198, R.D. #1
Odessa, New York 14869
U.S.A.
Born February 7, 1937

Eric Hilton is a self-employed artist who designs for Steuben glass. He has taught at the Edinburgh College of Art and New York State College of Ceramics at Alfred University. Education: Edinburgh College of Art, B.F.A., M.F.A.; Moray House Teachers College, Edinburgh. Selected Major Exhibitions: *American Glass Now,* Toledo, 1972. Publications: Julie Hall. *Tradition and Change: The New American Craftsman.* New York: E.P. Dutton, 1977, p. 94.

Pavel Hlava
Czechoslovakia
Na Břeunorské pláni 2951/55
160 00 Praha 6-Břevnov
Czechoslovakia
Born June 25, 1924

Pavel Hlava is a free-lance glass designer with Rosenthal Studio Haus. Education: High School of Applied Arts, Železný Brod, 1939-1942; Academy of Applied Arts, Prague, 1943-1948; Royal College of Art, London, 1966. Selected Major Exhibitions: *Glass 1959,* Corning; *Böhmisches Glas der Gegenwart,* Hamburg, 1973-1974; *Modernes Glas,* Frankfurt, 1976; *Coburger Glaspreis,* Coburg, 1977. Publications: Geoffrey Beard, *International Modern Glass.* 1976, p. 229.

Franz Xaver Hoeller
Federal Republic of Germany
Mondstrasse 9
D-8000 Munich 90
Federal Republic of Germany
Born October 18, 1950

Franz Hoeller is a glassmaker. Education: Staatl. Glasfachschule Zwiesel, 1971-1973.

David R. Huchthausen
United States
Helenenstrasse 56
Baden bei Wien 2500
Austria

David Huchthausen is currently a visiting artist at J & L Lobmeyr, Vienna. Education: University of Wisconsin, B.S., 1974; Illinois State University, M.F.A., 1977; University of Applied Arts, Vienna, 1977-1978. Selected Major Exhibitions: *National Sculpture Competition,* LaGrange, Georgia, 1973; *Modernes Glas,* Frankfurt, 1976; *New American Glass,* Huntington Galleries, Huntington, West Virginia, 1976; *Glass and Porcelain of Austria,* 1978; *Glass America,* 1978.

Reinhold Johann Hunkeler
Switzerland
St. Alban-Tal 42, CH-4052 Basel
Switzerland
Born January 5, 1951

Reinhold Hunkeler, a scientific glassblower in different ateliers, has been a free-lance glass artist working in his own studio since 1976. Education: Basel Technical College.

Peter Hünner
Denmark
Kurlandsgade 30, I
2300 Copenhagen S
Denmark
Born January 14, 1954

Mr. Hünner, an independent studio artist and assistant at the Skolen for Brugskunst, has designed for Snogebaek Glashytte, Bornholm, and is presently translating *Glas Håndbogen* by Finn Lynggaard into English. Selected Major Exhibitions: *Nordisk Glas 78,* Växjö; Stockholm, Sweden.

Robert Hurlstone
United States
712 North Greenwood
Park Ridge, Illinois 60068
U.S.A.
Born June 3, 1952

Mr. Hurlstone is an instructor of glass and three-dimensional design at Bowling Green State University. Education: Illinois State University, B.S., 1974; Southern Illinois University, M.F.A., 1978.

Ulrica Hydman-Vallien
Sweden
36063 Eriksmåla
Åfors
Sweden
Born March 24, 1938

Ulrica Hydman-Vallien works on a free-lance basis for Kosta-Boda. Education: Konstfackskolan, Stockholm, 1958-1961. Selected Major Exhibitions: Heal's, London, April 1974. Publications: Geoffrey Beard. *International Modern Glass.* London: Barrie and Jenkins, 1976.

Ichendorfer Glashütte
mbH
P.O. Box 3148
D-5010 Bergheim 3
Federal Republic of Germany

Ichendorfer was founded in 1907 and has 100 employees.

Kent F. Ipsen
United States
11761 Bowling Brook Drive
Richmond, Virginia 23235
U.S.A.
Born January 4, 1933

Ipsen is Professor at the School of Arts, Virginia Commonwealth University. Education: University of Wisconsin-Milwaukee, B.S., 1961; University of Wisconsin-Madison, M.S., 1964. M.F.A., 1965. Selected Major Exhibitions: *Objects: U.S.A.,* Washington D.C., 1969; *American Glass Now,* Toledo, 1972; *Glass America, 1978,* New York.

Ada Isensee
Federal Republic of
Germany
Eduard-Hiller-Str. 24 D-7064
Buoch
Federal Republic of Germany
Born May 12, 1944

Ada Isensee has been a free-lance designer since 1972. Education: École des Beaux Arts, Paris; Staatl. Akademie d. Bild. Kunste, Stuttgart; University Tübingen and Munich.

Vladimír Jelínek
Czechoslovakia
U Okrouhliku 2,
150 00 Praha 5-Košiře
Czechoslovakia
Born February 5, 1934

Jelínek is a free-lance glass designer. He designed for Karolinka Glassworks, 1961-1964. Education: High School of Applied Arts in Glass; Kamenický Senov, 1949-1952; Academy of Applied Arts, Prague, 1952-1958. Selected Major Exhibitions: *Böhmisches Glas der Gegenwart,* Hamburg, 1973-1974; *Modernes Glas,* Frankfurt, 1976; *Glaskunst der Gegenwart,* Kassel, 1977; *Coburger Glaspreis,* Coburg, 1977. Publications: Geoffrey Beard. *International Modern Glass.* 1976.

Jiří Jetmar
Czechoslovakia
Na Hrobci 1, 128 00 Prague 2–
Vinohrady
Czechoslovakia
Born September 7, 1950

Jiří Jetmar is a free-lance glass designer. Education: High School of Applied Arts (Glass), Železný Brod, 1965-1969; Academy of Applied Arts, Prague, 1969-1977; Hochschule für angewandte Kunst, Vienna, 1975-1976. Selected Major Exhibitions: *Czech Contemporary Glass,* Prague, 1977.

Jan Johansson
Sweden
AB Orrefors Glasbruk
S-380 40 Orrefors
Sweden
Born September 22, 1942

Jan Johansson has been a free-lance designer with Orrefors since 1975. Education: Swedish State School of Art and Design, Stockholm, 1963-1969.

Willy Johansson
Norway
Hadelands Glassverk
2700 Jevnaker Norway
Born May 2, 1921

Willy Johansson has been a designer with the Hadelands Glassverk since 1947. Education: State School of Applied Arts and Crafts, Oslo, 1939-1942. Selected Major Exhibitions: *Triennale,* Milan, 1954-1957; *Coburger Glaspreis,* Coburg, 1977.

Kagami Crystal Glass
Works Ltd.
12-23, 1-Chome Nishirokugo
Ota-ku, Tokyo
Japan

Kagami employs 240 people. The company specializes in glassware, dining utensils, items for interior decoration, and artistic products.

Benjamin Kaiser
United States/Israel
P.O. Box 126
San Jose, California 95103
U.S.A.
Born July 2, 1943

Mr. Kaiser, now a graduate student at San Jose State University, was instructor in a glassblowing program at Bezalel Academy of Art and Design, Jerusalem, Israel, from 1972-1974. Education: San Jose State University, B.A., 1977.

Marian Karel
Czechoslovakia
Tichá 2 150 00
Praha 5-Smíchov
Czechoslovakia
Born August 21, 1944

Mr. Karel is a free-lance glass designer. Education: High School of Applied Arts in Glass, Jablonec nad Nisou, 1959-1963; Academy of Applied Arts, Prague, 1966-1972. Selected Major Exhibitions: *Böhmisches Glas der Gegenwart,* Museum für Kunst und Gewerbe, Hamburg, 1976; *Coburger Glaspreis,* Coburg, 1977.

Peter Kaspar
Federal Republic of
Germany
Weinbergweg 2
6951 Neckarzimmern
Federal Republic of Germany
Born September 1, 1944

Mr. Kaspar is owner and manager of Glashütte Peter Kaspar, and has worked at Heesen-Glaswerke, Oberursel, and Gral-Glas, Dürnau. Education: Staatl. Glasfachschule, Zwiesel, 1966-1968. Selected Major Exhibitions: *Coburger Glaspreis,* Coburg, 1977.

Erzsébet Katona
Hungary
Hegyalja Ut 63
1124 Budapest
Hungary
Born November 19, 1942

Mrs. Katona has been a designer for Ferunion, exporters of Hungarian glassware, since 1962. Education: School for Applied Arts, Budapest, 1957-1962. Selected Major Exhibitions: *Coburger Glaspreis,* Coburg, 1977.

**Kyoichiro Kawakami
Japan**
*No. 2-8-3 Kyobashi
Chuo-ku, Tokyo
Japan
Born September 28, 1933*

Mr. Kawakami is design manager of Hoya Corporation. Education: Tokyo University of Fine Arts, 1956. Selected Major Exhibitions: *Glass '78 in Japan,* Odakyu Department Store, Tokyo, 1978.

**Robert Kehlmann
United States**
*2207 Rose Street
Berkeley, California 94709
U.S.A.
Born March 9, 1942*

Robert Kehlmann is a glass artist whose articles include "Schaffrath: Stained Glass and Mosaic," *Craft Horizons,* February 1978. Education: Antioch College, B.A., 1963; University of California, Berkeley, M.A., 1966. Selected Major Exhibitions: Habatat Gallery, Dearborn, Michigan, 1975; *New Stained Glass,* New York, 1978. Publications: Otto B. Rigan. *New Glass.* San Francisco: San Francisco Book Company Inc., 1976, pp. 91-93.

**Kerry Joe Kelly
Canada**
*532 Fisgard Street
Victoria, British Columbia
Canada
Born May 19, 1945*

Kerry Kelly is a stained glass artist. Selected Major Exhibitions: Habatat Gallery, Dearborn, Michigan, 1975. Publications: Otto B. Rigan, *New Glass.* San Francisco: San Francisco Book Company, Inc., 1976, p. 8.

**Russell K. Kelly
United States**
*9860 Rosebloom Avenue
Felton, California 95018
U.S.A.
Born June 28, 1947*

Russell Kelly is presently a student at San Jose State University. Education: Santa Barbara City College, A.A.; San Jose State University, B.A.

**Jesper Kerrn-Jespersen
Denmark**
*Kidedalsvej 21
DK-3460 Birkerød
Denmark
Born January 21, 1947*

Jesper Kerrn-Jespersen has worked alone in his own glass studio since 1974. Education: Orrefors Glassschool, 1973-1974. Selected Major Exhibitions: *Hot Glass,* London, 1976; *Coburger Glaspreis,* Coburg, 1977.

**Günter Knye
German Democratic
Republic**
*6426 Lauscha, Köppleinstrasse 67
German Democratic Republic
Born May 18, 1936*

Günter Knye is a glass artist and lampworker. Education: Trade examination, 1968; Fachschule für angewandte Kunst, Schneeberg, 1970-1972. Selected Major Exhibitions: Quadrennial Exhibition of Art Trade of the Socialist Countries, Erfurt I, 1974. II, 1978; *Glaskunst in der DDR,* Leipzig, 1977; *Coburger Glaspreis,* Coburg, 1977.

**Ernst Krebs
Federal Republic of
Germany**
*Marschnerstr. 82 D-8000 Munich
Federal Republic of Germany
Born April 11, 1939*

Ernst Krebs has been a free-lance artist since 1968. Education: Staatl. Fachschule für Glas und Schmuckwaren-Neugablonz, 1953-1956; Staatl. Glasfachschule, Zwiesel, 1956-1957; Akademie der bildenden Künste Munchen, 1957-1962. Selected Major Exhibitions: *Coburger Glaspreis,* Coburg, 1977.

**David Kroeger
United States**
*Box 25
Good Thunder, Minnesota 56037
U.S.A.
Born February 24, 1949*

David Kroeger is the owner of the Sasglameric Glass and Ceramics Studio.

Jon Kuhn
United States
162 Greenville Avenue
Staunton, Virginia 24401
U.S.A.
Born July 10, 1949

Mr. Kuhn operates Kuhn Art Glass Studio. Education: Washburn University, B.F.A.; Virginia Commonwealth University, M.F.A. Selected Major Exhibitions: *Contemporary Paperweights,* Habatat Galleries, Dearborn, Michigan, 1977.

Adolf Stepanovich Kurilov
USSR
Profsoyuznaya Street No. 76
Union Art Industrial Factory
Moscow, USSR
Born July 21, 1937

Adolf Stepanovich Kurilov has worked as an artist at the Guseusky glass factory since 1968 and has been a member of the Artist's Union of the USSR since 1970. Education: Moscow Higher Art Industrial Secondary School, 1968. Selected Major Exhibitions: *On Lenin's Way,* All-Union exhibition, 1977. Publications: L. Kazakova. *Gus Khrustal'nyi.* Moscow: Sovetskii Khdozhnik, 1973.

Dominick Labino
United States
Box 430
Grand Rapids, Ohio 43522
U.S.A.
Born December 4, 1910

Labino was Vice-president and Director of Research, Johns-Manville, and holds patents on glass compositions, processes, and machines. Education: Carnegie Institute of Technology; Toledo Museum of Art School of Design. Selected Major Exhibitions: *Objects U.S.A.,* Washington D.C., 1969; *American Glass Now,* Toledo, 1972; *Modernes Glas,* Frankfurt, 1976. Publications: Dominick Labino. *Visual Art in Glass.* Dubuque, Iowa; William C. Brown and Co., 1968.

Robert Levin
United States
Penland School of Crafts
Penland, North Carolina 28765
U.S.A.
Born September 25, 1948

Robert Levin is a resident craftsman at the Penland School of Crafts. Education: Denison University, 1971, B.F.A.; Southern Illinois University, M.F.A., 1974. Selected Major Exhibitions: *New American Glass: Focus West Virginia,* Huntington, West Virginia, 1976; *Young Americans: Clay/Glass,* New York, 1978. *North Carolina Glass, '78,* Cullowhee, North Carolina. Publications: *Glass Art Magazine,* No. 3, 1976.

Stanislav Libenský
Czechoslovakia
Brodec 645
468 22 Železný Brod
Czechoslovakia
Born March 27, 1921

Libenský, Professor at the Academy of Applied Arts, Prague, since 1965, was glass designer at the Železnobrodské sklo glassworks from 1949 to 1954 and Director of the High School of Applied Arts in Glass, Železný Brod from 1954 until 1965. Education: High School of Applied Arts in Glass, Železný Brod, 1937-1939; The Academy of Applied Arts, Prague, 1939-1944. Selected Major Exhibitions: *Glass 1959,* Corning, 1959; *Modernes Glas,* 1976; *Coburger Glaspreis,* 1977.

Walt Lieberman
United States
44 De Haven Drive
Yonkers, New York 10703
U.S.A.
Born January 1, 1954

Walt Lieberman is a free-lance glass artist. Education: Carnegie-Mellon University; Massachusetts College of Art, B.F.A.

Marvin Lipofsky
United States
1012 Pardee
Berkeley, California 94710
U.S.A.
Born September 1, 1938

Lipofsky, currently president of the Glass Art Society, is chairman of the Glass Department at California College of Arts and Crafts. He has designed glass for Venini and Leerdam. Education: University of Illinois, B.F.A., 1961; University of Wisconsin-Madison, M.S., M.F.A., 1964. Selected Major Exhibitions: *Objects U.S.A.,* Washington D.C., 1969; *American Glass Now,* Toledo, 1972; *Modernes Glas,* Frankfurt, 1976.

Věra Lišková
Czechoslovakia
Polská 54, 120 00
Praha 2-Vinohrady
Czechoslovakia
Born September 20, 1924.

Věra Lišková is a free-lance glass designer who has worked with Lobmeyr and Moser glassworks. Education: State Graphic School and Academy of Applied Arts, Prague, 1942-1949. Selected Major Exhibitions: *Expo '67,* Montreal; *Böhmisches Glas der Gegenwart,* Museum für Kunst und Gewerbe, Hamburg, 1974; *Coburger Glaspreis,* Coburg, 1977. Publications: Geoffrey Beard. *International Modern Glass.* London: Barrie and Jenkins, 1976, pp. 37, 234, 305.

Harvey K. Littleton
United States
Route 1, Box 843
Spruce Pine, North Carolina
28777
U.S.A.
Born June 14, 1922

Harvey Littleton is a self-employed sculptor in glass. He directed the 1962 glass workshop in Toledo and taught at the University of Wisconsin-Madison from 1951-1977. Education: Brighton School of Art, Great Britain, 1945; University of Michigan, 1947, B.D.; Cranbrook Academy of Art, 1951, M.F.A. Selected Major Exhibitions: *Objects U.S.A.,* Washington D.C., 1969; *American Glass Now,* Toledo, 1972; *Glas heute, Kunst oder Handwerk?* 1972; *Modernes Glas,* 1976.

J & L Lobmeyr
Kärntnerstrasse 26
A-1015 Vienna
Austria

Lobmeyr was founded in 1823 and has 72 employees. It specializes in copper wheel engraved glass, crystal chandeliers, and tableware.

Finn Lynggaard
Denmark
Ådalsvej 40
2970 Hørsholm
Denmark
Born January 11, 1930

Finn Lynggaard is Professor of Glass, School of Arts and Crafts, Copenhagen. Education: De Kgl. Akademiet for de Skonne Kunster, Copenhagen, 1951-1956. Selected Major Exhibitions: *XII. Triennale,* Milan, 1961; *Modernes Glas,* Frankfurt, 1976; *Coburger Glaspreis,* Coburg, 1977. Publications: Finn Lynggaard. *Glas Hånd-bogen.* Copenhagen: J. Fr. Clausens Forlag, 1975.

Václav Machač
Czechoslovakia
Jungmannova 212
394 70 Kamenice nad Lipou
Czechoslovakia
Born March 12, 1945

Mr. Machač is presently a teacher at the High School of Applied Arts in Glass, Nový Bor. Education: High School of Applied Arts in Glass, Železný Brod, 1959-1963; Academy of Applied Arts, Prague, 1965-1971. Selected Major Exhibitions: *Böhmisches Glas der Gegenwart,* Museum für Kunst und Gewerbe, Hamburg, 1973.

Marianne Maderna
Austria
Zeltgasse 12
1080 Wien
Austria
Born March 6, 1944

Marianne Maderna is a free-lance sculptor who has done book illustrations and designs for glass chandeliers. Education: Textilfachschule, Vienna, 1958-1959; Akademie für bildende Künste, Vienna, 1969-1972. Selected Major Exhibitions: *Coburger Glaspreis,* Coburg, 1977.

Peter Mansell
England
42 Hazell Road
Farnham, Surrey
Great Britain
Born June 30, 1951

Peter Mansell is presently Head Glassblower and Workshop Supervisor at Hirst Research Center. Education: Guilford Technical College.

Federica Marangoni
Italy
Dorsoduro 2615
Venice, Italy
Born August 24, 1940

Federica Marangoni has an architectural and design studio in Venice. Since 1976 she has taught summer courses and seminars for the New York University Art Department. Selected Major Exhibitions: *Biennale,* Venice, 1970; *The Art of Glass,* Brussels, 1973; *XV Triennale,* Milan, 1973.

Paul Marioni
United States
1712 Elm Avenue
Richmond, California 94805
U.S.A.
Born July 19, 1941

Paul Marioni is an independent glass artist. Education: University of Cincinnati, B.A. Selected Major Exhibitions: *New Stained Glass,* New York, 1978. Publications: Narcissus Quagliata. *Stained Glass from Mind to Light.* San Francisco: Mattole Press, 1976, pp. 192, 194, 220-230. Otto Rigan. *New Glass.* San Francisco: San Francisco Book Company, Inc., 1976, pp. 5-7.

Emilija Marodić
Yugoslavia
11 000 Beograd
Braće Jugovicá 23/VI
Yugoslavia
Born March 22, 1952

Mrs. Marodić is an independent glass artist who has designed for the Serbian glass factory in Paraćin since 1975. Education: Academy of Decorative Arts, Belgrade, 1975. Selected Major Exhibitions: *3. Triennale for Ceramics,* Museum for Applied Arts, Belgrade, 1977; *Coburger Glaspreis,* Coburg, 1977.

Richard Marquis
United States
1800-4th Street
Berkeley, California 94710
U.S.A.
Born September 17, 1945

Richard Marquis is in charge of ceramics and glass at the University of California, Los Angeles, and owner of Marquis Deluxe Studios. Education: University of California at Berkeley, B.A., M.A. Selected Major Exhibitions: *Objects U.S.A.,* Washington D.C., 1969; *American Glass Now,* Toledo, 1972; *Glass America, 1978,* New York. Publications: Julie Hall. *Tradition and Change: The New American Craftsman.* New York: E.P. Dutton, 1977.

Michel Martens
Belgium
Zeeweg 65
B-8200 Brügge
Belgium
Born March 21, 1921

Michel Martens is a self-taught glass artist who makes stained glass, murals, and mirror sculptures. Selected Major Exhibitions: *Coburger Glaspreis,* Coburg, 1977. Publications: "The Art and Technique of Stained Glass, The example of Michel Martens," *L'Art d'Eglise,* 1953, Nr. 4.

Paolo Martinuzzi
Italy
Fond. Navagero 57
Murano, Venezia
Italy
Born June 17, 1933

Paolo Martinuzzi has worked in glass factories in Milan and Murano. Selected Major Exhibitions: *Biennales,* Venice, 1970, 1972; *Glas heute, Kunst oder Handwerk?* Zurich, 1972; *Coburger Glaspreis,* Coburg, 1977; *Glaskunst der Gegenwart,* Kassel, 1977.

Tom McGlauchlin
United States
2527 Cheltenham
Toledo, Ohio 43606
U.S.A.
Born September 14, 1934

Tom McGlauchlin is instructor of glassblowing at The Toledo Museum of Art. Education: University of Wisconsin, 1954-1960, B.S., M.S.; University of Iowa, 1962. Selected Major Exhibitions: *Objects U.S.A.,* Washington D.C., 1969; *American Glass Now,* Toledo, 1972; *New American Glass: Focus West Virginia,* Huntington Galleries, 1976; *Glass America, 1978,* New York. Publications: Julie Hall. *Tradition and Change: The New American Craftsman.* New York, 1977.

Richard Craig Meitner
United States
Nieuwe Leliestraat 129
NL Amsterdam
Netherlands
Born January 3, 1949

Richard Meitner is a studio glass artist who has done free-lance work at Royal Leerdam, Netherlands. Education: University of California, Berkeley, 1970-1972; Gerrit Rietveld Akademie, Amsterdam, 1972-1975. Selected Major Exhibitions: *Coburger Glaspreis,* Coburg, 1977.

Mária Mészáros
Hungary
Szerüskert 39
Budapest 1046
Hungary
Born December 26, 1949

Mária Mészáros is a free-lance glass artist. Education: Academy of Applied Arts, Budapest, 1977.

Floris Meydam
Netherlands
Laantje van van Iperen 15
NL Leerdam
Netherlands
Born December 29, 1919

Floris Meydam is Chief Designer for United Glassworks and Royal Leerdam. He has designed objects for the "Unica" series. Education: Glasschool Leerdam, 1943. Selected Major Exhibitions: *Glass 1959,* Corning, 1959; *Modernes Glas,* Frankfurt, 1976; *Coburger Glaspreis,* Coburg, 1977; *Glaskunst der Gegenwart,* Kassel, 1977.

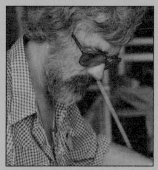

Steven Mildwoff
United States
Milropa Studios Inc.
85-25 126th Street
Kew Gardens, New York 11415
U.S.A.

Klaus Moje
Federal Republic of
Germany
Kirchwerder Hausdeich 370
D-205 Hamburg 80
Federal Republic of Germany
Born October 5, 1936

Peter Mollica
United States
1940-a Bonita Avenue
Berkeley, California 94704
U.S.A.
Born December 26, 1941

Nancy D. Monk
United States
7305 College Avenue, Apt. B
Whittier, California 90602
U.S.A.
Born August 1, 1951

Steven Mildwoff, president of Milropa Studios Inc., was vice-president of Bent Glass Works Inc., New York, and has taught glassworking at the New School for Social Research. Education: Art Students League, New York; Academy of Art, Florence. Selected Major Exhibitions: *Glass 1959,* Corning, 1959; Toledo Glass Nationals I and II, Toledo, 1966 and 1968; *Glass America, 1978,* New York, 1978.

Since 1962, Klaus Moje has operated an independent glass studio with Isgard Moje. Education: Staatl. Glasfachschule Rheinbach, 1952-1956; Staatl. Glasfachschule Hadamar, 1957-1959. Selected Major Exhibitions: *Modernes Glas,* Frankfurt, 1976; *Coburger Glaspreis,* Coburg, 1977.

Peter Mollica has had his own stained glass studio since 1968. Education: Study with Chris Rufo (1964-1968), Ludwig Schaffrath, and Patrick Reyntiens (1974). Selected Major Exhibitions: *California Contemporary Stained Glass,* Fresno, 1976; *New Stained Glass,* New York, 1978. Publications: Otto Rigan. *New Glass.* San Francisco: San Francisco Book Company, Inc., 1976. pp. 10-12; Narcissus Quagliata. *Stained Glass from Mind to Light.* San Francisco: Mattole Press, 1976. pp. 207-213.

Nancy Monk was a drawing instructor at Minneapolis College of Art and Design, 1976-1977. Education: Colorado State University, B.F.A.; University of Minnesota, M.F.A.

Benjamin Moore
United States
9702 Hunter Point Road N.W.
Olympia, Washington 98502
U.S.A.
Born February 5, 1952

Roberto Moretti
United States
53 Rolland Park Drive
Huntington, West Virginia 25700
U.S.A.
Born September 16, 1930

R. Scott Mundt
United States
4084 Piedmont Avenue, Apt. 2
Oakland, California 94615
U.S.A.
Born August 10, 1954

Sue Murray
Scotland
Nuthanger, Cargill,
Perth, Scotland
United Kingdom
Born January 25, 1947

Benjamin Moore, who has worked for Fostoria Glass Company, now designs for Venini, Murano, Italy, and is on the faculty of the Pilchuck Glass Center. Education: California College of Arts and Crafts, B.F.A.; Rhode Island School of Design, M.F.A. Selected Major Exhibitions: Museum of Contemporary Crafts, New York.

Roberto Moretti is a master craftsman at the Pilgrim Glass Company in Ceredo, West Virginia. Education: Technical School of Glass Design, Murano, Italy. Selected Major Exhibitions: Huntington Galleries, Huntington, West Virginia.

Scott Mundt is a graduate student at the California College of Arts and Crafts. Education: University of Wisconsin-Stevens Point; Tyler School of Art, B.F.A.

Sue Murray is a self-employed lampworker. Education: Edinburgh College of Art; Royal College of Art, London; Isleworth Polytechnic. Selected Major Exhibitions: *European Lampworkers,* Lobmeyr, Vienna.

Jay Musler
United States
273 22nd Avenue A
San Francisco, California 94121
U.S.A.
Born March 18, 1949

Jay Musler has been a professional glassblower at Maslach Art Glass Co., Greenbrae, California, for six years. Education: California College of Arts and Crafts.

Joel Philip Myers
United States
R.R. 2, Bunn Street Road
Bloomington, Illinois 61701
U.S.A.
Born January 29, 1934

Joel Myers is Professor of Art at Illinois State University. From 1963 to 1970 he was Director of Design, Blenko Glass, Milton, West Virginia. Education: Parsons School of Design, New York, 1951-1954; Kunsthaandvaerkerskolen, Copenhagen, 1957-1958; New York State College of Ceramics, Alfred University, B.F.A., M.F.A. 1960-1963. Selected Major Exhibitions: *Objects U.S.A.,* Washington D.C., 1969; *Glas heute, Kunst oder Handwerk?* 1972; *Modernes Glas,* 1976.

Paul Neuman
United States
1129 Lexington Avenue
New York, New York 10021
U.S.A.
Born March 3, 1954

Paul Neuman is an independent studio glass artist. Education: New York State College of Ceramics, Alfred University, B.F.A. 1977. Selected Major Exhibitions: *Young Americans Clay/Glass,* Museum of Contemporary Crafts, New York, 1978.

John Henry Nickerson
United States
720 Front Street
Louisville, Colorado 80027
U.S.A.
Born May 15, 1939

John Nickerson, design director at Blenko Glass Co., Milton, West Virginia, from 1970-1974, is a self-employed artist-craftsman. Education: Montana State University, B.S. 1964; Alfred University, M.F.A. 1969.

James R. Nieswaag
United States
7471 Van Buren Street, N.E.
Minneapolis, Minnesota 55432
U.S.A.
Born May 25, 1957

Education: Anoka Ramsey Community College, A.A.

Břetislav Novák, Jr.
Czechoslovakia
468 22 Železný Brod 669
Czechoslovakia
Born February 8, 1952

Břetislav Novák, Jr. is a free-lance glass designer. Education: High School of Applied Arts in Glass, Železný Brod, 1967-1971; Academy of Applied Arts, Prague, 1972-1978. Selected Major Exhibitions: *Böhmisches Glas der Gegenwart,* Hamburg, 1973-1974; *Coburger Glaspreis,* Coburg, 1977.

Ladislav Oliva
Czechoslovakia
Vaněčkova 431/53
468 22 Železný Brod
Czechoslovakia
Born August 21, 1933

Ladislav Oliva has taught at the High School of Applied Arts in Glass, Železný Brod, since 1969. From 1957 to 1964 he designed at the Borské sklo glassworks, and from 1964 to 1969 at the Bohemia glassworks, Podebrady. Education: High School of Applied Arts in Glass, Kamenický Šenov, 1948-1951. Academy of Applied Arts, Prague, 1951-1957. Selected Major Exhibitions: *Glass 1959,* Corning; *XII Triennale,* Milano, 1960; *Böhmisches Glas der Gegenwart,* Hamburg, 1973-1974.

Anthony Parker
United States
0416 SW Iowa Street
Portland, Oregon 97201
U.S.A.
Born July 17, 1945

Anthony Parker was an instructor at Portland State University from 1973 to 1976. Education: Portland State University, B.S. 1972; M.F.A. 1976. Selected Major Exhibitions: *Glass of the Northwest,* White Gallery, Portland State University, 1975.

Thomas Patti
United States
Main Road
Savoy, Massachusetts 01256
U.S.A.
Born October 16, 1943

Thomas Patti is an independent glass artist and director of the Savoy Glass School. Education: Pratt Institute, B.I.D., M.I.D. Selected Major Exhibitions: *Glass America, 1978,* New York, 1978.

Mark Peiser
United States
Penland, North Carolina 28765
U.S.A.
Born January 8, 1938

Mark Peiser is an independent glass artist. Education: Purdue University; Illinois Institute of Technology; De Paul University, School of Music. Selected Major Exhibitions: *Objects: U.S.A.,* Washington, 1969; *American Glass Now,* Toledo, 1972; *Glass America, 1978,* New York; *North Carolina Glass, '78,* Cullowhee, North Carolina.

Ronald Pennell
England
2 Lower Bibbletts
Hoarwithy, Hereford HR 2-6QF
United Kingdom
Born May 26, 1935

Ronald Pennell, an engraver, is Crafts Adviser to the International African Institute. Education: Moseley School of Art; Birmingham College of Art.

Robert E. Pietruszewski
United States
1845 West 33rd Avenue
Denver, Colorado 80211
U.S.A.
Born November 17, 1950

Robert Pietruszewski is currently studying in Poland on a Fullbright Grant. He has worked at the Denver Arts Workshop and is presently with Artel Glass Studios, Denver. Education: University of Wisconsin-Madison, B.A. 1978. Selected Major Exhibitions: *Frozen Fluid: Ideas in Glass,* Elvehjem Art Center, Madison, Wisconsin, 1978.

The Pilgrim Glass
Corporation
Airport Road
Ceredo, West Virginia 25507
U.S.A.

The Pilgrim Glass Corporation was founded in 1950 and employs 110 people. It specializes in handcrafted, mouth blown crystal and hand sculptured art objects.

Oldřich Plíva
Czechoslovakia
Mšeno 165, 466 04 Jablonec nad Nisou
Czechoslovakia
Born April 17, 1946

Oldřich Plíva is a free-lance glass designer. Education: High School of Applied Arts in Glass, Železný Brod, 1960-1964; Academy of Applied Arts, Prague, 1965-1971. Selected Major Exhibitions: *Böhmisches Glas der Gegenwart,* Hamburg, 1973-1974.

Dionisie Popa
Romania
Str. N. Iorga Nr. 42
Bucharest 7000
Romania
Born May 19, 1938

Dionisie Popa is a free-lance artist and member of the Union of Romanian Artists. Education: Institut für Bildende Künste, Nicolae Grigorescu, Bucharest, 1971-1976. Selected Major Exhibitions: *Coburger Glaspreis,* Coburg, 1977.

Richard Posner
United States
c/o Robert Posner, Box 327
Canyon Dam, California 95923
U.S.A.
Born August 16, 1948

Richard Posner is artist-in-residence (1977-1978) at the Exploratorium, San Francisco. He has taught at the Pilchuck Glass Center (1973) and the California College of Arts and Crafts (1975-1976). Education: Chico State College, B.A., 1973; California College of Arts and Crafts, M.F.A., 1976. Selected Major Exhibitions: *New Stained Glass,* New York, 1978. Publications: Otto Rigan. *New Glass.* San Francisco: San Francisco Book Company, Inc., 1976, pp. 98-99.

Narcissus Quagliata
United States
1360 Howard Street
San Francisco, California 94103
U.S.A.
Born May 2, 1942

Narcissus Quagliata is a stained glass artist and the author of *Stained Glass from Mind to Light.* Education: San Francisco Art Institute, B.F.A., 1966; M.F.A., 1968. Selected Major Exhibitions: *New Stained Glass,* New York, 1978. Publications: Otto Rigan. *New Glass.* San Francisco: San Francisco Book Company, Inc., 1976, pp. 20-22.

Rastal-Werk
Lindenstreet P.O. Box 215
D-5410 Höhr-Grenzhausen
Federal Republic of Germany

Rastal-Werk was founded in 1919 and employs 650 people. The firm specializes in the production of glass, ceramics, and pewter.

Astri Reusch
Canada
4421 Avenue de l'Esplanade
Montreal, Quebec H2W 1T2
Canada
Born April 8, 1945

Astri Reusch is a self-taught glass artist. Education: Ecole des Beaux-arts de Montreal; Montreal Museum of Fine Arts; Concordia University, Montreal. Selected Major Exhibitions: Canadian Guild of Crafts, Montreal, 1977.

Claus Josef Riedel
Tiroler Glashütte GmbH
A-6332 Kufstein, Weissachstr.
Austria

The Riedel factory was founded in 1756 and employs 300 people. The company specializes in the production of lead crystal.

Rochester Folk Art Guild
R.D. 1, Box 10
Middlesex, New York 14507
U.S.A.

The Rochester Folk Art Guild, founded in 1957, specializes in traditional crafts. In 1975 it had 50 members.

Rosenthal
Aktiengesellschaft
Hauptabteilung
Verkaufsförderung D-8672 Selb
(Bayern)
Federal Republic of Germany

Rosenthal was founded in 1879 and employs 584 people. It specializes in handblown glass.

Daniel Alan Rothenfeld
United States
19100 South Park Boulevard
Shaker Heights, Ohio 44122
U.S.A.
Born November 29, 1953

Daniel Rothenfeld is a self-employed glassblower. Education: Rhode Island School of Design, B.F.A. 1977.

Miluše Roubíčková
Czechoslovakia
Laubova 10, 130 00
Prague 3-Vinohrady
Czechoslovakia
Born July 20, 1922

Miluše Roubíčková is a free-lance glass designer. Education: High School of Applied Arts, Prague, 1941-1943; Academy of Applied Arts, Prague, 1943-1949. Selected Major Exhibitions: XI and XII *Triennale,* Milano, 1957, 1960; *Böhmisches Glas der Gegenwart,* Hamburg, 1973-1974; *Coburger Glaspreis,* Coburg, 1977.

Ivo Rozsypal
Czechoslovakia
Bezručova 69
473 01 Nový Bor
Czechoslovakia
Born August 12, 1942

Ivo Rozsypal has been a glass designer with the Crystalex glassworks since 1973; he designed for the Borské sklo glassworks, Nový Bor, 1963-1966. Education: High School of Applied Arts in Glass, Kamenický Šenov, 1959-1961; Academy of Applied Arts, Prague, 1966-1973. Selected Major Exhibitions: *Contemporary Czechoslovak Glass,* Prague, 1977.

Cristalería San Carlos
S.A.
San Martin 1646
3013 San Carlos Centro (SFE)
Argentina

Cristalería San Carlos was founded in 1949 and employs 200 people. Its products include lead crystal, colored glass, tableware, and general household glassware.

Laura de Santillana
Italy
San Marco 3328
Venice
Italy
Born May 12, 1955

Laura de Santillana is a free-lance designer who has worked with Vignelli Associates and Venini in Italy. Education: School of Visual Arts, New York.

Fumio Sassa
Japan
No. 2-8-3 Kyobashi
Chuo-Ku, Tokyo
Japan
Born February 16, 1924

Fumio Sassa is General Manager and Director of Hoya Corporation. Education: National Institute of Industrial Arts and Technics, 1944. Selected Major Exhibitions: *Brussels International Fair,* Brussels, 1958.

No photograph
available.

Lubov Ivanovna Savelieva
USSR
Profsoyuznaya Street No. 76
Union Art Industrial Factory
Moscow, USSR
Born January 14, 1940

Lubov Ivanovna Savelieva is a free-lance artist who has worked with decorative glass since 1966. She has been a member of the Artist's Union of the USSR since 1970. Education: Moscow Higher Art Industrial Secondary School, 1966. Selected Major Exhibitions: *On Lenin's Way,* All-Union exhibition, 1977. Publications: N. Voronov, E. Rachuk. *Soviet Glass.* Leningrad: Aurora Art Publishers, 1973.

Albin Schaedel
German Democratic
Republic
Plaueschestr. 15
5210 Arnstadt/Thür
German Democratic Republic
Born 1905

Albin Schaedel has had his own workshop since 1954. Education: Trained in his father's workshop; studied with Professor Karl Staudinger. Selected Major Exhibitions: *Glass 1959,* Corning, 1959; *Modernes Glas,* Frankfurt, 1976; *Coburger Glaspreis,* Coburg, 1977; *Glaskunst in der DDR,* Leipzig, 1977. Publications: *Albin Schaedel Lampengeblasenes Glas,* Leipzig, 1970 (Exhibition catalog); Ada Polak. *Modern Glass.* London: Faber and Faber Limited, 1962, p. 74.

Otto Hans Schaffer
Federal Republic of
Germany
Dreilindenstr. 1a
6232 Bad Soden-Neu
Federal Republic of Germany
Born January 7, 1942

As a glass cutter, Otto Schaffer has run his own glass shop and workshop since 1975. Education: Glass Technical School, West Germany.

Bernhard Schagemann
Federal Republic of
Germany
Rachelstr. 14, 8372 Lindberg
Federal Republic of Germany
Born March 2, 1933

Bernhard Schagemann has been a glass artist since 1970. He has taught at the Staatl. Fachschule für Glas, Zwiesel, since 1970. Education: Academy of Arts, Munich, 1954-1957, 1959-1960. Selected Major Exhibitions: *Coburger Glaspreis,* Coburg, 1977.

Jack A. Schmidt
United States
11141 East Blvd., University Circle
Cleveland, Ohio 44106
U.S.A.
Born December 1, 1945

Jack Schmidt is visiting instructor at The Cleveland Institute of Art. Education: Bowling Green State University, B.S. 1968; Illinois State University, M.S. 1973. Selected Major Exhibitions: *American Glass Now,* Toledo, 1972; *New American Glass: Focus West Virginia,* Huntington Galleries, Huntington, West Virginia, 1976; *Glass America, 1978,* New York.

Paul Schulze
United States
Steuben Glass, Corning Glass Works
Corning, New York 14830
U.S.A.
Born February 7, 1934

Paul Schulze is Director of Design at Steuben Glass. Education: New York University, B.S.; Parsons School of Design.

Eric Sealine
United States
Kenwyn Apts. 1-B
Wynnefield and 50th
Philadelphia, Pa. 19100
U.S.A.
Born December 7, 1948

Eric Sealine is a professional artist. Education: Iowa State University, B.S. 1970.

Paul Seide
United States
85-25 126th Street
Kew Gardens, New York 11415
U.S.A.
Born February 15, 1949

Paul Seide is head designer and co-founder of Milropa Studios, Inc. From 1976 to 1977 he taught glassmaking at the New School for Social Research. Education: University of Wisconsin-Madison, B.S.; Egani School of Neon Glass Technology, New York. Selected Major Exhibitions: *Glass America, 1978,* New York, 1978.

Theodor G. Sellner
Federal Republic of Germany
D-8371 Bayr. Eisenstein
Regenhütte 54
Federal Republic of Germany
Born January 5, 1947

Theodor Sellner is a free-lance glass artist. Education: Glasfachschule Zwiesel, 1961-1964. Selected Major Exhibitions: *Coburger Glaspreis,* Coburg, 1977.

Randy Sewell
United States
5650 Main Street
Bethania, North Carolina 27010
U.S.A.
Born July 25, 1944

Randy Sewell is the proprietor of Stained Glass of Bethania. From 1973 to 1975 he was associate director, Pounds Stained Glass Inc., New Orleans, Louisiana. Education: Huntingdon College, B.S., 1969; Ohio University, M.F.A, 1972. Selected Major Exhibitions: *Biennial Exhibition of Piedmont Crafts,* Mint Museum of Art, Charlotte, North Carolina, 1978.

Mary Shaffer
United States
17 Edgehill Road
Providence, Rhode Island 02906
U.S.A.
Born October 3, 1947

Mary Shaffer is a self-employed sculptor who has taught at various universities including the University of Rhode Island, the University of Massachusetts (Amherst) and the University of Chicago (Artist-in-residence). Education: Rhode Island School of Design, B.F.A.; Ecole d'Humanite, Goldern, Switzerland. Selected Major Exhibitions: *Glass America, 1978,* New York.

Donald A. Shepherd
United States
49 Old N. Stamford Road
Stamford, Connecticut 06905
U.S.A.
Born October 9, 1930

Donald Shepherd is a designer for Blenko Glass Company and Design Director, D.A.S. Designs. He was formerly a design consultant to Libbey Glass Company, 1973-1976. Education: California School of Fine Arts, 1953-1957; Catan-Rose Institute of Fine Arts, New York, 1953-1957.

Josh Simpson
United States
Frank Williams Road
Shelburne Falls, Mass. 01370
U.S.A.
Born August 17, 1949

Josh Simpson is a full-time glass artist. Education: Hamilton College, B.A., 1972. Selected Major Exhibitions: *Young Americans Clay/Glass,* New York, 1978.

Rolf Sinnemark
Sweden
Boda Bruks AB
360 65 Boda glasbruk
Sweden
Born September 20, 1941

Rolf Sinnemark is a designer for Kosta Boda. Education: HKS Konstfakskolan, Stockholm.

Vratislav Šotola
Czechoslovakia
Řásnovka 6, 110 00 Praha 1
Staré Město
Czechoslovakia
Born May 9, 1931

Since 1955, Vratislav Šotola has been a glass designer in the Center of Home Culture, Prague. Education: High School of Applied Arts in Glass, Kamenický Šenov and Nový Bor, 1946-1949; Academy of Applied Arts, Prague 1949-1954. Selected Major Exhibitions: *Glass 1959,* Corning, 1959; *XII Triennale,* Milan, 1960.

Mark Stanley
United States
119 North 4th Street
Minneapolis, Minnesota 55401
U.S.A.
Born May 15, 1951

Mark Stanley was visiting artist at Les Verriere de Ile D'Mars, Grenoble, France, in 1977. Education: St. Cloud State College, B.A., 1972; University of Minnesota, M.F.A., 1977.

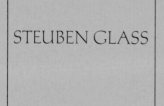

Steuben Glass
Corning Glass Works
Corning, New York 14830
U.S.A.

Steuben Glass, founded in 1903, employs 250 people and specializes in lead crystal objects, both functional and decorative, hand-blown and engraved.

Hans Gottfried von
Stockhausen
Federal Republic of
Germany *Eduard-Hiller-Str. 24*
D-7064 Buoch
Federal Republic of Germany
Born May 12, 1920

Von Stockhausen is Professor of Glass Design at the Staatl. Akademie der Bildenden Künste, Stuttgart (since 1970); he has been a free-lance painter and glass designer since 1951. Education: Staatl. Akademie der Bildenden Künste, Stuttgart, 1947-1951. Selected Major Exhibitions: *Mille Ans d'Art du Vitrail,* Strassbourg, 1965; *Coburger Glaspreis,* Coburg, 1977; *Glaskunst der Gegenwart,* Kassel, 1977.

Michelle Hope Stuhl
United States
c/o Gider 1190 N.E. 163rd Street
North Miami Beach, Fla. 33162
U.S.A.
Born July 11, 1957

Michelle Stuhl is a professional sculptress. Education: University of Wisconsin-Madison, B.S. Selected Major Exhibitions: *Ideas in Glass,* Elvehjem Art Center, Madison, Wisconsin, 1978.

Jiří Šuhájek
Czechoslovakia
Americka 20
360 00 Karlovy Vary
Czechoslovakia
Born April 14, 1943

Jiří Šuhájek has been a glass designer in the Moser Glassworks (Karlovy Vary) since 1972. Education: High School of Applied Arts in Glass, Kamenický Šenov, 1957-1961; Academy of Applied Arts, Prague, 1964-1968; Royal College of Art, London, 1968-1971. Selected Major Exhibitions: *Böhmisches Glas der Gegenwart,* Hamburg, 1973-1974; *Modernes Glas,* Frankfurt, 1976. Publications: J. Hetteš. "Arts and Crafts and Glass Production." *Glass Review,* No. 9/74, pp. 2-7.

Susquehanna Glass Company
731 Avenue H
Columbia, Pennsylvania 17512
U.S.A.

Susquehanna Glass was founded in 1910. The company employs 70 and specializes in handcut glassware.

Denji Takeuchi
Japan
2-6, 2-chome,
Nihonbashi-Bakuro-Cho
Chou-Ku, Tokyo, Japan
Born May 4, 1934

Denji Takeuchi is design department manager and designer with Sasaki Glass Mfg. Co. Ltd, Tokyo. Education: Kyoto University of Art and Science, 1958. Selected Major Exhibitions: *Glass 78 in Japan,* Odakyu Department Store, Tokyo, 1978.

Dalibor Tichý
Czechoslovakia
Na pískách 5/674
160 00 Praha 6-Dejvice
Czechoslovakia
April 21, 1950

Dalibor Tichý is presently a glass designer at "Crystalex" glassworks, Nový Bor. Education: High School of Applied Arts in Glass, Kamenický Šenov, 1965-1970; Academy of Applied Arts, Prague, 1970-1976. Selected Major Exhibitions: *Böhmisches Glas der Gegenwart,* Hamburg, 1973-1974; *Contemporary Czechoslovak Glass,* Prague, 1977.

Inkeri Toikka
Finland
Oy Wärtsilä AB
31160 Nuutajärvi
Finland
Born December 14, 1931

Inkeri Toikka is a designer for Nuutájarvi Glass. Education: Drawing School of Turku Arts Association; Apprenticeship at Kupittaan Savi, 1950-1952; Institute of Industrial Art, Department of Ceramics, Helsinki, 1952-1955.

Joaquin Torres Esteban
Spain
Jorge Juan, 86
Madrid 9
Spain
Born October 20, 1919

Mr. Esteban is director of the Torres y Begue Art Gallery and was artistic and promotional director of the Cortes Ingles department store chain. Education: Circulo de Bellas Artes de Madrid. Selected Major Exhibitions: International Gallery, New York; *Coburger Glaspreis,* Coburg, 1977.

Kapka Toušková
Bulgaria (working in Czechoslovakia)
Bartákova 1117 140 00 Praha 4,
Pankrác Czechoslovakia
Born February 10, 1940

Kapka Toušková is a free-lance glass designer. Education: High School of Fine Arts, Sofia, 1954-1959; Academy of Fine Arts, Sofia, 1960-1963; Academy of Applied Arts, Prague, 1963-1966. Selected Major Exhibitions: *Böhmisches Glas der Gegenwart,* Hamburg, 1974.

Karla Trinkley
United States
311 Harrison Avenue
Elkins Park, Pennsylvania 19117
U.S.A.
Born July 31, 1956

Karla Trinkley is a student at the Tyler School of Art. Education: Bucks County Community College, A.A.

Bertil Vallien
Sweden
Åfors 360 63 Eriksmåla
Sweden
Born January 17, 1938

Bertil Vallien is a designer-artist with Kosta-Boda, Sweden. Education: Konstfackskolan, Stockholm. Selected Major Exhibitions: Stedleijk Museum, Holland; National Museum, Stockholm.

**Mark Edward Vance
United States**
*P.O. Box 99
Peninsula, Ohio 44264
U.S.A.
Born April 26, 1947*

Val-Saint-Lambert
*Rue de Val, 245
4100 Seraing
Belgium*

**Aleš Vašíček
Czechoslovakia**
*Na Spojce 8
101 00 Praha 10 Vršovice
Czechoslovakia
Born February 22, 1947*

**Jorma Vennola
Finland**
*14500 Iittala
Finland
Born April 24, 1943*

Mark Vance has operated Vance Glassworks since September 1974. Education: Bowling Green State University, B.S., M.A., M.F.A.

Val-Saint-Lambert was established in 1825. It specializes in cut and engraved glass and artware.

Aleš Vašíček is a free-lance glass designer. Education: High School of Applied Arts in Glass, Železný Brod, 1962-1966; Academy of Applied Arts, Prague, 1966-1972. Selected Major Exhibitions: *Böhmisches Glas der Gegenwart,* Hamburg, 1973-1974; *Coburger Glaspreis,* Coburg, 1977.

Jorma Vennola has been a product designer at Iittala glassworks since 1975. He has worked for Corning Glass Works (1973-1975) and Creative Playthings (1970-1973). Education: Institute of Industrial Design, Helsinki, 1970.

**Robert Vesely
United States**
*289 State Street
Portland, Maine 04101
U.S.A.
Born December 28, 1949*

**Zsuzsa Vida
Hungary**
*Galgoosy ut 1916
1125 Budapest
Hungary
Born April 13, 1944*

**Sylvia B. Vigiletti
United States**
*20300 North Greenway
Southfield, Michigan 48076
U.S.A.*

Vignelli Associates
*410 East 62nd Street
New York, New York 10021
U.S.A.*

Robert Vesely is a self-employed artist. Education: Cleveland State University, B.A.; Cranbrook Academy of Art, M.F.A.

Zsuzsa Vida teaches at the College of Applied Arts in Budapest. Education: Academy of Applied Arts, VSUP, Prague, 1966.

Sylvia Vigiletti is a studio artist in glass and Treasurer of the Glass Art Society. Education: Wayne State University; Center for Creative Studies, College of Art and Design, Detroit, Michigan. Selected Major Exhibitions: *Contemporary Art Glass '76,* New York, 1976; *National Paperweight Exhibition,* Habatat Galleries, Dearborn, Michigan, 1977.

Vignelli Associates was established in New York in 1971 by Massimo and Lella Vignelli. It is involved in graphic design, interiors, furniture, glass and other products. Vignelli glass designs are manufactured by Heller Designs.

František Vízner
Czechoslovakia
Zelenohorská 42
591 02 Žďár nad Sázavou II
Czechoslovakia
Born March 9, 1936

František Vízner has been a free-lance glass artist since 1975. From 1961 until 1967 he designed for the Dubi glassworks (near Teplice) and from 1967 to 1974 for the Skrdlovice glassworks. Education: High School of Applied Arts in Glass, Nový Bor, 1951-1953; High School of Applied Arts in Glass, Železný Brod; Academy of Applied Arts, Prague, 1956-1962. Selected Major Exhibitions: *Böhmisches Glas der Gegenwart,* Hamburg, 1973-1974; *Coburger Glaspreis,* 1977.

Ann Wärff
Sweden
Transjö 360 52
Kosta
Sweden
Born February 26, 1937

Ann Wärff has been a designer at Kosta Boda, Sweden, since 1964. From 1960 to 1964 she designed at Pukebergs Glassworks, Nybro, Sweden. Education: Hamburg, Zürich, and the Hochschule für Gestaltung, Ulm. Selected Major Exhibitions: *Modernes Glas,* Frankfurt, 1976; *Coburger Glaspreis,* Coburg, 1977. Publications: Geoffrey Beard. *International Modern Glass.* London: Barrie and Jenkins, 1976, p. 250, plates 5, 150, 151.

Mary Warren
United States
5477 College Avenue
Oakland, California 94618
U.S.A.
Born April 8, 1956

Mary Warren is presently an apprentice to Richard Posner. Education: California College of Arts and Crafts, B.A., 1978.

Steven I. Weinberg
United States
34 Winoka Drive
Huntington Station, N.Y. 11746
U.S.A.
Born June 4, 1954

Steve Weinberg is a working artist and a student at the Rhode Island School of Design. Education: New York State College of Ceramics, Alfred University, B.F.A., 1976. Selected Major Exhibitions: *Young Americans Clay/Glass,* New York, 1978; *Glass America, 1978,* New York.

David Kerr Whittemore
United States
c/o Dirks, 50-1/2 Barrow Street
New York, New York 10014
U.S.A.
Born June 3, 1926

David Whittemore has taught glass at the School of Visual Arts, New York. Education: Fleisher Art Memorial, Philadelphia; Hunter College, New York; Art Students League, New York. Selected Major Exhibitions: *Toledo Glass National,* Toledo, 1966.

David Willard
United States
29 Blue Bill Park Drive
Madison, Wisconsin 53718
U.S.A.
Born May 9, 1948

David Willard is head of the glass program at the University of Wisconsin-Madison. Education: Cranbrook Academy of Art, B.F.A., 1974; Tyler School of Art, M.F.A., 1976. Selected Major Exhibitions: *Fragile Art,* Glass Masters Guild, 1978; *Young Americans, Clay/Glass,* New York, 1978.

Willet Stained Glass
Company
10 East Moreland Avenue
Philadelphia, Pennsylvania
19118
U.S.A.

Willet Stained Glass was founded in 1890 and employs 60 people. Its specialty is stained and faceted glass, gold windows, and farbigem glass (a chemical lamination).

Regina Wlodarczyk-
Puchała
Poland
Osiedle Huty 10b
58-580 Szklarska Poreba Poland
Born September 24, 1931

Regina Wlodarczyk-Puchała has been working at the Julia Crystal glass factory in Szklarska, Poreba since 1958. Education; Art Academy, Wrocław, 1952-1958. Selected Major Exhibitions: General Polish Glass Exhibition in Katowice, 1974, 1977; *Coburger Glaspreis,* Coburg, 1977.

Alina Wolowska
Poland
Chopina 7/54
00559 Warsaw
Poland
Born September 3, 1923

Wilfried Zaglauer
Federal Republic of
Germany
Reichertsriederstr. 13 D-8371
Kirchberg
Federal Republic of Germany
Born September 26, 1947

Jiřina Žertová
Czechoslovakia
U Železné lávky 10
118 00 Praha 1-Malá Strana
Czechoslovakia
Born August 13, 1932

Yan Zoritchak
Czechoslovakia
(working in France)
Bluffy, 74290 Veyrier du Lac
France
Born November 13, 1944

Designer Alina Wolowska began working in glass in 1968. She works part-time at a state-owned glassworks; Ms. Wolowska has also made glass for historical movies. Education: University of Warsaw, M.A., 1968. Selected Major Exhibitions: *Coburger Glaspreis,* Coburg, 1977.

Wilfried Zaglauer is a glass designer at F. X. Nachtmann KG, Riedlhütte, West Germany. Education: Zeichenakademie Hanau, 1964-1966; Glasfachschule Zwiesel, 1971-1974.

Jiřina Zertová has been a free-lance glass designer since 1955. Education: State School of Graphic Arts, Prague, 1947-1950; Academy of Applied Arts, Prague, 1950-1955. Selected Major Exhibitions: *Böhmisches Glas der Gegenwart,* Hamburg, 1973-1974; *Coburger Glaspreis,* Coburg, 1977.

Yan Zoritchak is a free-lance artist and sculptor who has designed for Daum and Baccarat in France, Val St. Lambert in Belgium, and in Czechoslovakia. Education: School of Glass, Železný Brod; High School of Craft Arts, Prague. Selected Major Exhibitions: *Coburger Glaspreis,* Coburg, 1977.

Index

Index by Nationality

Norway

1. Johansson, Willy

Poland

1. Wlodarczyk-Puchała, Regina
2. Wolowska, Alina

Romania

1. Băncilá, Dan
2. Popa, Dionisie

Spain

1. Torres Esteban, Joaquin

Sweden

1. Backström, Monica
2. Branzell, Arne
3. Cyrén, Gunnar
4. Forsell, Ulla
5. Gille, Marianne
6. Hellsten, Lars
7. Hydman-Vallien, Ulrica
8. Johansson, Jan
9. Sinnemark, Rolf
10. Vallien, Bertil
11. Wärff, Ann

Switzerland

1. Hunkeler, Reinhold Johann

United Kingdom
England

1. Clarke, Dillon
2. Cook, John Heald
3. Cowdy Glass Workshop Limited
4. Esson, Michael D. (working in Australia)
5. Flavell, Ray
6. Mansell, Peter
7. Pennell, Ronald

United Kingdom
Scotland

1. Hilton, Eric (working in U.S.A.)
2. Murray, Sue

United States

1. Anchor Hocking Corporation
2. Armbruster, Tom
3. Babcock, Herbert
4. Bartron, Paula
5. Ben Tré, Howard
6. Bernstein, Rick
7. Bernstein, William
8. Block, Jonathan
9. Burton, John
10. Castellan, Diane H.
11. Chihuly, Dale
12. Clarke, James
13. Cmarik, Robert
14. Cohn, Michael
15. Conover, Jamie L.
16. Dailey, Dan
17. Dexter, William
18. Dowler, David
19. Duggan, Richard
20. Fräbel, Hans Godo
21. Giberson, Dudley F.
22. Gilmor, John D.
23. Grossman, J. R.
24. Halem, Henry
25. Handler, Audrey
26. Harmon, James R.
27. Harned, Richard Spencer
28. Huchthausen, David R.
29. Hurlstone, Robert
30. Ipsen, Kent
31. Kaiser, Benjamin
32. Kehlmann, Robert
33. Kelly, Russell K.
34. Kroeger, David
35. Kuhn, Jon
36. Labino, Dominick
37. Levin, Robert
38. Lieberman, Walt
39. Lipofsky, Marvin
40. Littleton, Harvey K.
41. Marioni, Paul
42. Marquis, Richard
43. McGlauchlin, Tom
44. Meitner, Richard Craig
45. Mildwoff, Steven
46. Mollica, Peter
47. Monk, Nancy D.
48. Moore, Benjamin
49. Moretti, Roberto
50. Mundt, R. Scott
51. Musler, Jay
52. Myers, Joel Philip
53. Neuman, Paul
54. Nickerson, John Henry
55. Nieswaag, James R.
56. Parker, Anthony
57. Patti, Thomas
58. Peiser, Mark
59. Pietruszewski, Robert E.
60. Pilgrim Glass Corporation, The
61. Posner, Richard
62. Quagliata, Narcissus
63. Rochester Folk Art Guild
64. Rothenfeld, Daniel Alan
65. Schmidt, Jack A.
66. Schulze, Paul
67. Sealine, Eric
68. Seide, Paul
69. Sewell, Randy
70. Shaffer, Mary
71. Shepherd, Donald A.

72. Simpson, Josh
73. Stanley, Mark
74. Steuben Glass
75. Stuhl, Michelle Hope
76. Susquehanna Glass Company
77. Trinkley, Karla
78. Vance, Mark Edward
79. Vesely, Robert
80. Vigiletti, Sylvia B.
81. Vignelli Associates
82. Warren, Mary
83. Weinberg, Steven I.
84. Whittemore, David Kerr
85. Willard, David
86. Willet Stained Glass Company

U.S.S.R.
1. Kurilov, Adolf Stepanovich
2. Savelieva, Lubov Ivanovna

Yugoslavia
1. Marodić, Emilija

Objects Exhibited in Corning Only

The following objects, with the initials of the judges who chose them, were shown only in the Corning exhibition, April 26, 1979– October 1, 1979. They are not illustrated in the catalog.

274. Jan Adam, *Drop II,* December 1977, PS

275-277. Paula Bartron, *Lustred Bottle with Stopper,* Spring, 1978, RL, WS, PS; *Lustred Bottle with Tree/Grass Stopper,* Spring 1978, WS, PS; *Matt-etched Brown Bottle with Stopper,* Spring, 1978, FS-G

278. Howard Ben Tré, *Burial Box: Type I Blue,* December 1977, PS

279. Rick Bernstein, *Drip Dry'd Lips,* February 1978, RL, WS

280, 281. William Bernstein, *Storm and Seed Series,* 1977, WS; *Reflection,* 1977, WS

282, 283. Dale Chihuly, *Evato Serape, 1976,* PS; *Opal Basket,* 1977, RL

284. Jamie L. Conover, *Teeny Mureeni,* March 1978, PS

285, 286. Daum & Cie, *Coppelia 52,* 1977, WS; *Coppelia 33,* Made January 1978, Designed January 1978, FS-G

287. David Dowler, *Reflective Object #2,* January 1977, FS-G, PS

288. Antonín Drobník, *Ado I,* February 1978, WS

289. J. R. Grossman, *Pooh-Dog's #8,* 1977, WS

290-293. James R. Harmon, *DV1504,* October 1977, WS, PS; *2020 CSDV,* November 1977, RL, WS, PS; *2011 LPRDV,* WS, PS; *2011 CSDV,* November 1977, FS-G, WS

294. Pavel Hlava, *Blue Crystal,* November 1977, PS

295. Peter Hünner, *Torvegade 75,* February 1978, FS-G, PS

296. Robert Hurlstone, *Untitled,* January 1978, RL, PS

297, 298. Ulrica Hydman-Vallien, *Pink Animal with Black Rat,* 1978, WS; *Flowers on Pokal,* 1978, RL

299. Kent Ipsen, *Copper Ruby Jar,* June 1976, PS

300. Marian Karel, *Crystal,* June 1977, FS-G, RL, WS

301. Marvin Lipofsky, *Broken Basket Form,*

Holding Series 1978, 1978, PS

302. Harvey K. Littleton, *Lavender Sliced Form,* 1977, PS

303. Richard Marquis, *Faceted Lightning and Star Cup Form,* March 1978, RL, PS

304. Richard Craig Meitner, *Vase,* October 1977, WS

305. Nancy D. Monk, *Mississippi on My Mind,* 1977, PS

306. Joel Philip Myers, *Untitled (scent bottle),* 1977, PS

307, 308. Thomas Patti, *Clear Band,* 1978, PS; *Planular Rib,* 1977, PS

309. Mark Peiser, *Moon and Pines OP37,* 1977, PS

310. Ronald Pennell, *Married Bliss,* 1977, PS

311, 312. Cristalería San Carlos S.A., *Pote Chiriguano 349–Llamas Relief,* Made January 1978, Designed September 1976, WS; *Pote 155–Winged Snake Relief,* Made September 1976, Designed September 1976, WS

313. Jack A. Schmidt, *Ten Degree Break,* December 1977, PS

314. Dalibor Tichý, *Sunset,* November 1977, RL, WS

315. Bertil Vallien, *Trumpet Blower in Sand Unik 4201,* January 2, 1978, WS

316. Mark Edward Vance, *Vase II,* October 1977, WS

317. František Vízner, *Smoked Vase,* March 1978, FS-G, PS

Selected Bibliography

Anderson, Harriette. *Kiln-Fired Glass.* Philadelphia: Chilton Book Co., 1970.

Beard, Geoffrey. *International Modern Glass.* London: Barrie and Jenkins, 1976.

Beard, Geoffrey. *Modern Glass.* London: Studio Vista Ltd., Dutton Pictureback, 1968.

Berlye, Milton K. *The Encyclopedia of Working with Glass.* Dobbs Ferry, New York: Ocean Publications, 1968.

Burton, John. *Glass: Philosophy and Method, Hand-Blown, Sculptured, Colored.* Philadelphia: Chilton Book Co., 1967.

Coburg. Kunstsammlungen der Veste Coburg. *Coburger Glaspreis 1977 für Moderne Glasgestaltung in Europa.* Coburg: The Museum, 1977.

Cologne. Kunstgewerbemuseum. *Wagenfeld, Wilhelm. 50-Jahre Mitarbeit in Fabriken.* Cologne: The Museum, 1973.

Cologne. Kunsthaus am Museum (Carola van Ham). *Glas Heute.* Cologne: The Gallery, 1973.

Contemporary Art Glass Group and The Glass Art Society. *Contemporary Art Glass '76.* New York: 1976.

Contemporary Art Glass Group and The Glass Art Society. *Glass America, 1978.* New York: 1978.

Coral Gables, Florida. Lowe Art Museum, University of Miami. *International Glass Sculpture.* Coral Gables, Florida: The Museum, 1973.

The Corning Museum of Glass. *Contemporary Glass, 1976.* (Color microfiche with text). Corning: The Museum, 1977.

The Corning Museum of Glass. *Contemporary Glass, 1977.* (Color microfiche with text). Corning: The Museum, 1978.

The Corning Museum of Glass. *Glass 1959: A Special Exhibition of International Contemporary Glass.* Corning, New York: The Museum, 1959.

The Corning Museum of Glass. *A Survey of Glassmaking from Ancient Egypt to the Present.* Compiled by Charleen Edwards. (Color microfiche with text). Chicago and London: University of Chicago Press, 1977.

Crafts Advisory Committee. *Working with Hot Glass; Papers from the International Glass Conference.* London: Royal College of Art, 1977.

Cullowhee, North Carolina. Art Gallery, Western Carolina University. *North Carolina Glass, '74.* Cullowhee, North Carolina: The Museum, 1974.

Cullowhee, North Carolina. Art Gallery, Western Carolina University. *North Carolina Glass, '76.* Cullowhee, North Carolina: The Museum, 1976.

Cullowhee, North Carolina. Art Gallery, Western Carolina University., *North Carolina Glass, '78.* Cullowhee, North Carolina: The Museum, 1978.

Dallas. Museum of Fine Arts. *Air, Light, Form: New American Glass.* Dallas, Texas: The Museum, 1967.

Darmstadt. Hessisches Landesmuseum. *Glaskunst im Bann der Farbe.: I. Arte nova–Techniken der Glashütte.* Darmstadt: The Museum, 1976. II. *Vor der Lampe geblasenes Glas.* Darmstadt: The Museum, 1978.

Düsseldorf. Kunstmuseum. *Leerdam Unica: 50 Jahre modernes niederlandisches Glas.* Düsseldorf: The Museum, 1977.

Flavell, Ray and Smale, Claude. *Studio Glassmaking.* New York: Van Nostrand Reinhold Co., 1974.

Frankfurt am Main. Museum für Kunsthandwerk. *Modernes Glas aus Amerika, Europa und Japan.* Frankfurt: The Museum, 1976.

Glass–an Old Friend. Exhibition of International Studio Glass. Copenhagen, s.n.: 1975.

Glass [Art Magazine] Vol. 1, 1973 to date.

Glass Review. Czechoslovak Glass and Ceramic Magazine, Vol. 1, 1946 to date.

Grover, Ray and Lee. *Contemporary Art Glass.* New York: Crown Publishers Inc., 1975.

Hall, Julie P. *Tradition and Change: The New American Craftsman.* New York: E. P. Dutton, 1977.

Hamburg. Museum für Kunst und Gewerbe. *Böhmisches Glas der Gegenwart.* Hamburg: The Museum, 1973.

Hammesfahr, James E. and Clair L. Strong. *Creative Glass Blowing.* San Francisco: W. H. Freeman, 1968.

Heddle, G. M. *A Manual on Etching and Engraving Glass.* London: Alex Tiranti, 1961.

Hieke, Wilhelm. *Glasschliff und Glasgravur.* Bamberg: Verlagshaus Meisenbach KG, 1969.

Huntington, West Virginia. Huntington Galleries. *New American Glass: Focus West Virginia.* Part 1–The Glassblowing Process. Part 2–Exhibition Catalog.* Part 3–Off-hand Glass for Production. Part 4–Glass Workshop Project. Huntington, West Virginia: The Museum, 1976.

Isenberg, Anita and Seymour. *How to Work in Stained Glass.* Philadelphia: Chilton Book Co., 1972.

Janneau, Guillaume. *Modern Glass.* London: The Studio Limited, 1931.

Janneau, Guillaume. *Le Verre et l'art de Marinot.* Paris: Floury, 1925.

Japan Glass Artcrafts Association. *Glass '78 in Japan.** Odakyu Department Store. Tokyo: Asahi Shinbun?, 1978.

Kassel. Hessischen Landesmuseum. *Glaskunst der Gegenwart.* Kassel: The Museum, 1977.

Kinney, Kay. *Glass Craft: Designing, Forming, Decorating.* Philadelphia: Chilton, 1962.

Koch, Robert. *Louis C. Tiffany, Rebel in Glass.* New York: Crown Publishers Inc., 1964.

Kulasiewicz, Frank. *Glassblowing: the Technique of Free-Blown Glass.* New York: Watson-Guptill, 1974.

Labino, Dominick. *Visual Art in Glass.* Dubuque, Iowa: William C. Brown Company, 1968.

Liège. Musée du Verre. *Verrerie Européenne 1958-1963.** Liège: The Museum, 1963.

Leipzig. Museum des Kunsthandwerks. *Glaskunst in der DDR.** Leipzig: The Museum, 1977.

Littleton, Harvey K. *Glassblowing, A Search for Form.* New York: Van Nostrand Reinhold Co., 1971.

Long Beach, California. Long Beach Museum of Art. *Reflections on Glass.** Long Beach, California: The Museum, 1971.

Lynggaard, Finn. *Glas Håndbogen.* Copenhagen: J. Fr. Clausens Forlag, 1975.

Metcalf, Robert and Gertrude. *Making Stained Glass: A Handbook for the Amateur and the Professional.* New York: McGraw-Hill, 1972.

Modern Bohemian Glass. Introductory text by J. Raban. Biographical data and catalog by A. Matura. Texts written in cooperation with L. Smrčkova, B. Stiess and J. Kotík. Translated by Ota Vojtíšek. Prague: Artia, 1963.

Newman, Harold. *An Illustrated Dictionary of Glass, with an Introductory Survey of the History of Glassmaking by Robert J. Charleston.* London: Thames and Hudson, 1977.

New York. Museum of Contemporary Crafts. *Young Americans, Clay/Glass.** New York: American Crafts Council, 1978.

Nordness, Lee. *Objects U. S. A.* New York: Viking Press, 1970.

Norman, Barbara. *Engraving and Decorating Glass.* New York: McGraw-Hill, 1972.

O'Brien, Vincent. *Techniques of Stained Glass: Leaded, Faceted, and Laminated Glass.* New York: Van Nostrand Reinhold, 1977.

Perrot, Paul N. *A Short History of Glass Engraving.* New York: Steuben Glass, 1973.

Polak, Ada. *Modern Glass.* London: Faber and Faber, 1962.

Quagliata, Narcissus. *Stained Glass from Mind to Light.* San Francisco: Mattole Press, 1976.

Rigan, Otto B. *New Glass.* San Francisco: San Francisco Book Company, Inc., 1976.

Rothenberg, Polly. *The Complete Book of Creative Glass Art.* New York: Crown Publishers Inc., 1974.

Schuler, Frederic. *Flameworking: Glassmaking for the Craftsman.* Philadelphia: Chilton Book Co., 1968.

Schuler, Frederic and Lilli. *Glassforming: Glassmaking for the Craftsman.* Philadelphia: Chilton Book Co., 1970.

Stained Glass, A Quarterly of the Stained Glass Association of America. Vol. 1, 1906 to date.

Steenberg, Elisa. *Modern Swedish Glass.* Stockholm: Lindqvists, 1949.

Stennett-Wilson, Ronald. *The Beauty of Modern Glass.* London and New York: Studio, 1958.

Stennett-Wilson, Ronald. *Modern Glass.* New York: Van Nostrand-Rheinhold, 1975.

Toledo, Ohio. The Toledo Museum of Art. *Toledo Glass National I, 1966 *; Toledo Glass National II, 1968 *; Toledo Glass National III, 1970.* *Toledo: The Museum, 1966, 1968, 1970.

Toledo, Ohio. The Toledo Museum of Art. *American Glass Now.** Toledo, Ohio: The Museum, 1972.

Tooley, Fay VaNisle. *Handbook of Glass Manufacture; a Book of Reference for the Plant Executive, Technologist, and Engineer,* rev. ed. New York: Ogden Publishing Co., 1974.

Wausau, Wisconsin. The Leigh Yawkey Woodson Art Museum. *Americans in Glass: 1978.* Wausau, Wisconsin: The Museum, 1978.

Weyl, Woldemar A. *Coloured Glasses.* Sheffield: Society of Glass Technology, 1976. (Paperback reprint of 1951 edition).

Zurich. Museum Bellerive. *Glas Heute, Kunst oder Handwerk?** Zurich: The Museum, 1972.

*Exhibition catalog.

DATE